CREATIVITY

CREATIVITY

Concept and Findings

SHAMSHAD HUSSAIN

Foreword by

S.M. MOHSIN

MOTILAL BANARSIDASS

Delhi Varanasi Patna

Bangalore Madras

First Edition: Delhi, 1988

MOTILAL BANARSIDASS
Bungalow Road, Jawahar Nagar, Delhi 110 007
Branches
Chowk, Varanasi 221 001
Ashok Rajpath, Patna 800 004
24, Race Course Road, Bangalore 560 001
120 Royapettah High Road, Mylapore, Madras 600 004

ISBN: 81-208-0391-4

PRINTED IN INDIA
BY JAINENDRA PRAKASH JAIN AT SHRI JAINENDRA PRESS, A-45 NARAINA INDUSTRIAL AREA, PHASE I, NEW DELHI 110028 AND PUBLISHED BY NARENDRA PRAKASH JAIN FOR MOTILAL BANARSIDASS, DELHI 110007.

To

The Loving Memory of My Niece

SEEMA TABASSUM

A Fine Creation of

the Almighty Creator

CONTENTS

FOREWORD

Few problems concerning human abilities have been more enigmatic than that of creativity. In spite of engaging very serious attention of psychologists for about a little more than two decades now, not even a modicum of insight regarding its nature and source has so far been gained that could stand the rigor of a critical and empirical evaluation. Nevertheless, a plethora of research data generated by the attack on the problem from different angles, and even by different disciplines, lies in store for the researcher to grapple with it, and its documentation is the outstanding feature of Dr. Shamshad Hussain's book on Creativity: Concept and Findings. In this respect it serves as the most comprehensive book of reference relating to the subject. This is testified by the very exhaustive bibliography including about three hundred titles of books and journal articles published and even unpublished, in the eastern and western countries. It is by itself an important contribution, since the very highly elusive nature of the subject, should prevent the reader to expect a final say on it from any writer.

Among the five chapters of the book, the fourth one, dealing with the cross-cultural studies of creativity, also reports an investigation conducted by the author himself concerning a comparison between the results of Mehdi's test of creativity administered on a sample of tribal and that of non-tribal students of Ranchi which has produced very revealing significant findings. I am confident that Dr. Hussain's volume on creativity will provide very valuable source materials for future researches on the subject which is most likely to be captivating the interest of psychologists and critics of art and literature for some time to come.

S. M. MOHSIN

Ex-Prof. & Head,
Deptt. of Psychology,
Patna University, Patna.
Darulman/Patna, 16.1.87

PREFACE

The present age is characterized by confusion, tension and violence. The creative ability seldom gets proper channels for its utmost expression. The creative imagination of a child is lost amidst highly mechanical and routined life. This has posed a serious problem before the psychologists and the educationists. The creative potentials, present within a man, if not properly expressed through constructive channels, would generate suffocation and divert his creative ability towards destructive tendencies. If the constructive and imaginative endeavour is not properly catered it will generate more and more frustration within the individuals. Any blockage to creative expression on the part of human beings will lead to their psychological death. The human being who is the supreme creation of God may not justify the purpose of his existence which is meant for creating something novel on this earth and ultimately to add beauty to his Creator's gift.

The present educational system and unrealistic syllabi, are so taxing to the growing children that their creative imagination is suppressed and blocked most of the time. While speaking at an International Conference at Delhi in January, 1986, Dr. R. Ramanna, Chairman Atomic Energy Commission, has cast doubt over the contribution of formal education to creative development of children. He has posed a question: Are children being exposed to too much knowledge in the rapid advancing world today at the cost of stunting their creativity? The education must not only aim at intellectual development but also at creative expression.

Such discussions and arguments are indicative of the fact that creativity is an important subject for scientific investigation and empirical study. Various problems related to the proper expression of creative potentials need thorough discussion and exploration as well as understanding of the nature of creativity in its diversified forms. Only when the concept of creativity is fully understood in different contexts one can provide ways for its proper channelization.

The problem of defining creativity and distinguishing it from intelligence has been considered to be of such significance that for the last three to four decades investigators have been deeply interested in its study from conceptual and empirical angles. Psychologists have turned their deep interest to analysing the nature of creativity and to answering various questions related to its multi-dimensional character. Some of the important questions which have been raised are: What is, in fact, the true nature of creativity? Is it parallel to intelligence? Can it be explained in terms of process, product, person or press? Is every individual basically endowed with creative potentials? Do the creatives constitute a distinct and separate category of people? Does the formal education facilitate the expression of creative potentials or block it? Is creative work original and unique? What effect does a family or socio-cultural set-up make on the growth of creative ability? Do the creative individuals possess some distinguished personality traits or disposition ? What type of educational activities are needed for proper expression of hidden creative potentials?

Many other such questions have been raised by the investigators and diverse arguments have been put forward in support of one's reply to these questions. Various issues related to the study of creativity have, thus, generated interest in the educators and the investigator for its critical study. The complex nature of creativity and the diversified views on it attracted the present author to take up this issue again in the light of available documents.

The present book represents the author's effort at analysing the concept of creativity and also the various research findings available in this context. The book consists of five main chapters. Chapter I deals extensively with conceptual understanding of the term 'creativity' in the light of various approaches.

Chapter II is exclusively devoted to the study of creativity in the light of the controversies over its dependence on intelligence. An effort has been made to examine various approaches regarding the nature of relationship between creativity and intelligence. The main issue was to determine whether high intelligence leads to higher creativity. In spite of deep analysis of the subject the author still feels that further efforts are to be made in this direction.

Chapter III deals with the study of creativity in familial perspective. In the light of various empirical findings the contribution of familial undercurrents to the growth of individual's creativity has been examined. Factors like parental socio-economic status, their involvement in creative art, provision for proper incentives, family structure, liberal and conservative outlook, parental presence/absence, etc. have been taken into consideration as they affect creativity of children.

The subject for discussion in Chapter IV is the effect of cultural variables on the development of creative ability of the individuals. Various cross-cultural studies have been presented along with their interpretations in order to examine whether cultural heritage contribute to development of creativity in its members.

Chapter V exclusively deals with the issue whether creative individuals possess some distinguishable personality characteristic, as their work is characterized by the production of idea off the beaten track, 'outside the mold'. Various views regarding the nature of such traits have been quoted. An idea of these important differentiating traits may enable us to find the conditions in early life which give rise to them and the predisposition toward creative thinking. I hope fully that further research will discover some of the characteristics of family life which are important and fundamental in producing people with the personality characteristics of creative thinkers.

The references are up-to-date and cover even the latest literature on the subject. These references will help the researchers in obtaining detailed accounts of the findings, if they so desire.

On the whole, I have tried to present different views on creativity and analyse them in the light of empirical researches. I have incorporated a number of studies conducted in our country, as well as abroad, for the purpose of clarifying the concept of creativity and its various constituents.

I have not only collected the research materials available in this field but also have tried to assimilate and interpret them. At many places the readers will find my personal remarks and suggestions with regard to the research techniques and tools employed in the study of creativity.

I hope that the present book will be of some help to those who are interested in knowing something about the nature of creativity and the various problems associated with its interpretations. The book will, I trust, prove immensely useful especially to the researchers who are working in this area of creativity. It will enable the psychologists and the educationists to appreciate and understand various issues related to the proper growth of hidden creative potentials within children. The parents and teachers may be benefited by its study. Specially the chapter devoted to familial and social factors of creativity can contribute much to the understanding of the parents of their children's creative thirst. The findings given in the book would provide extensive knowledge regarding the contribution of intelligence, family, culture and personality variables towards an individual's creative endeavour. The research data may be utilized by the educated parents, teachers and researchers in their effort to develop a correct perspective of children's creativity. However, I feel that further efforts are to be made for arriving at some concrete conclusions regarding the nature of creativity which still remains highly controversial and therefore unresolved.

SHAMSHAD HUSSAIN

ACKNOWLEDGEMENT

I express my deep sense of gratitude to my respected teacher Dr. S.M. Mohsin, Retired Professor and Head of the Department of Psychology, Patna University, for associating himself with my present endeavour by writing a Foreword to the book. He has been all the time a source of inspiration to me and I consider him to be an 'academic saint'.

I owe my gratitude to Dr. B. De, Ex-Professor and Head of the Department of Psychology, Patna University for extending his valuable suggestions from time to time. It has been my privilege to incorporate his research findings in my book. I really like him for his intellectual as well as human qualities.

How can I forget Prof. L.N.K. Sinha, Head, Department of Psychology, Patna University, with whom I have often discussed various problems of research.

My personal indebtedness is to respected Prof. (Dr.) K.N. Prasad, the Ex-Vice Chancellor of Patna University, who has always encouraged and blessed me during odd moments of my life.

I do remember the blessings and encouragement of my revered teacher Dr. R.N. Sharma, Prof. T. Nath and Prof. R.C. Prasad of my department.

I feel indebted to my students Dr. S.M. Sajid and Dr. Pratima Sharan whom I supervised during their doctoral research, for making their sincere efforts towards analysing various problems related to creativity. I take it as my pleasure and privilege to incorporate their research findings in my book.

I am really very much obliged to Mr. Nayeem Haidri, U.G.C. teacher-fellow, working under me, for extending his constant assistance during the writings of the manuscript of the book.

I do remember Dr. Khursid Jehan a student and colleague of mine who rendered all possible help, as usual, in compiling different findings given in this book.

I must express my thanks to Dr. Baqer Mehdi, Professor of Education, N.C.E.R.T. New Delhi for extending his valuable suggestions from time to time.

ACKNOWLEDGEMENT

I express personal indebtedness to my wife Nishat Abdin who has been always very kind to encourage me in taking up such ventures by becoming personally involved.

I do acknowledge the blessings and love of my sisters Atia Khatoon and Shahina.

How can I forget to mention the name of Hesham Bhai and Mujeeb as well as that of my Najmi, Raunaque (a creative) and loving Hena who identify themselves with my pleasure and success. My sincere thanks and blessings are due to my Chhotan (M. Rahman) for taking personal interest in providing different aids and assitance to me during the writing of this book.

I shall be failing in my duty if I do not express my hearty gratitude to M/s Motilal Banarsidass for publishing the book. I am especially thankful to Shri Kamla Shankar Singh, Branch Manager, Motilal Banarsidass, Patna for showing his keen interest in the publication of this book. I also express my thanks to M. Rehman and Mr. Waseem Ansari for typing the manuscript of this book with all their sincerity.

What I miss at the time of writing this acknowledgement is the presence of my niece 'Seema Tabassum' whom I considered to be my ideal and source of inspiration. Recently she left us alone in this world and created a vacuum in our life. Now her loving kids, Iema, Shadab and Soma are source of inspiration to me. I do remember the loving presence of Zaidi, Faizi, Faisal and Tabish Babu who stand before me whenever I write such things and smile with pleasure. The presence of these kids in my home is enough for taking any intellectual pursuit.

While writing a book on creativity I am reminded of the high aesthetic sense of my revered teacher, late Prof. M.Z. Abdin, and late Md. Sulaiman (I.A.S.) for having great fascination for nature's creative gifts.

Last, but not the least, I remember my revered parents, Late Aulad Hussain and Ummat Fatima and my father-in-law late Moinul Abdin who are no more with me but their memories and image guide and bless me whenever I take up any intellectual work.

S.H.

CHAPTER ONE

CONCEPTUAL ANALYSIS OF CREATIVITY

Creation of man is the culmination of God's creative pursuit. The hidden and expressive endowment of this creativity in man reflects the creative endeavour of the Almighty creator. However, the true nature of creativity has not been fully understood as yet. Its nature is so complex that it still remains shrouded in mystery and efforts are to be made for unfolding its multi-dimensional character. The ways are to be paved for healthy expression of creative potentials with which human beings are endowed. If we fail to do so the potentially creative individual may start suffocating and divert his creative endeavour into destructive channels. That is why, the analysis of creativity from conceptual and empirical angles constitutes a subject of valuable investigation. Fortunately, people have realized the necessity for exploring the true nature of man's creativity, which is reflected in rich literature available on creativity. The review of such literature indicates that creativity has been examined in a conceptual as well as empirical context.

The findings associated with various problems of creativity are controversial in nature. Some have examined the concept of creativity from one angle whereas others from another. Different articles and research findings are coming up on this issue. On the whole, it has been noted that creativity as a concept is not easy to be defined. Various popular as well as highly technical definitions have been put forward in support of the nature of creativity. Creativity is to be analysed from a multi-dimensional approach as it is highly complex cognitive ability. The controversies regarding the agreed definition of creativity clearly suggest the multiplexity underlying the explanation of creative behaviour. If one starts collecting the various definitions of creativity, he will get confused. What is needed at present is to touch the fundamentals of creativity. The conceptual framework is to be provided in the light of various approaches to the analysis of creative behaviour. Findings in the area of creativity either by applying psycho-metric tools or by observing and analysing the actual creatives in the light of the creative talents, suggest that still extensive and intensive researches are needed for the purpose of exploring something concrete and convincing regarding the nature and manifestations of creativity.

In the light of above note, it seems proper to study creativity as a concept and also its manifestations in terms of creative performance. It is not to be studied in isolation as a cognitive mental process but in the context of various cognitive and non-cognitive factors which have their direct or indirect influence on the growth and development of creative potentials present in a man.

Creativity has not been scientifically defined as most of the definitions are ambiguous and have examined creativity in a loose term. Laymen have added more ambiguity while defining creativity. Various popular meanings of creativity have been put forward. The most popular way of looking at creativity has been to emphasize on the making of something 'new' and 'different'. Fromm (1959) has pointed out two broad meanings of creativity. First, it refers to the production of something novel and further it may even refer to the attitude which may persist even when nothing new is created.

Brunnelle (1970) has regarded creativity in terms of a process by which some novel idea or an object is produced in a new fashion or arrangement. In the absence of this process there cannot be any product and ultimately no creativity.

Kunt (1982) has also considered creativity as consisting of various processes like framing, probing, exploring, affirming and realizing. Through these processes the pursuer's relation to the phenomenon undergoes change and new insight is attained. All such definitions lay greater emphasis on the act of producing as central to the concept of creativity rather than on the end result of that. Psychologists like Mackinnon (1960), Dewey (1910), Wallas (1926) have also viewed creativity as a process leading to some new idea or object. The originality has been thus, widely emphasized while defining creativity. What is created is considered to be quite novel and differentiating from what already exists. Therefore, 'uniqueness' constitutes the fundamental characteristics of a creative product. Parker (1963) considers creativity as the art of seeking out, trying out and combining knowledge in a novel way which results in something new.

Goldner (1962) has stressed that creativity is an organized, comprehensive and imaginative activity of brain toward an original outcome. It is, therefore, an innovative and not a reproductive activity.

Mendick (1964) views creative thinking in the light of framing new combinations of associative elements which either meet specified requirement or is found to be useful in some way. The more mutual remote elements of the new combination, the more creative is the process.

However, criticisms are there against this common notion. Barron (1961) is of the opinion that creativity does not simply mean exploration, invention or discovery of some new things or relations rather it refers to making new combinations out of existing objects and elements.

Celye (1962) while recognizing one more dimension of creativity states that it leads to generalization of the new interpretations. These interpretations of creativity, in short, emphasize that creativity involves the combination of old ideas or products into new forms, but the old extends the base for the new ideas. As far as 'uniqueness' in creativity is concerned Hurlock (1978) has explained that 'uniqueness' is a personal achievement, not necessarily an universal one. For example, an individual may be creative when he produces something which he could not produce earlier, however, it may have been produced in almost the same, or even in identical form by some other individual.

In spite of some criticisms regarding the originality, novelty and uniqueness in creativity it is observed that there is still stress on creativity as an unique mental process which is needed for production of something novel and original.

Here one can also quote Guilford (1968) in support of originality, deviation and uniqueness in creativity. He has considered creativity as a specific kind of thinking; labelled as divergent thinking which makes deviation from the common and obvious thought and action. This type of thinking helps an individual in examining various possible solutions to a problem and not centring around a single correct solution which involves 'convergent' thinking. In convergent thinking the person follows the prevailing mode of thought, information and action to arrive at one right answer which could be attained by other individuals also. Divergent thinking enables the individual to be more flexible and fluent involving richer flow of ideas and resulting in some novel and creative solution.

Morgan (1953) also examined 25 definitions of creativity and he found that in spite of differences in opinion there is consensus that creativity involves the development of something unique, although the uniqueness in itself has not been defined in one way.

That is why it has been suggested that if one is interested in measuring the excellence in divergent thinking he has to consider all possible varied responses which can be produced by an individual and also the number of statistically unique responses. Guilford (1957-9) has clearly remarked that creativity can be measured through divergent thinking test.

Divergent thinking abilities represent an individual's intellectual operation where he is free to choose a new direction or perspective on a given subject. In this thought process the stored information is scanned, possible solutions are searched and thought flows in diversified direction, which help the individual in penetrating into a new and untested direction. In creative thinking also the matter is generated from the memory storage but there are possibilities to solve a problem by linking new connections or by adopting revised forms which ultimately leads to the production of something new and unique which is considered to be an important condition for creative work.

Divergent thinking includes fluency, flexibility, originality, elaboration and also evaluative abilities. An examination of various tests of divergent thinking has revealed that the responses are generally interpreted in terms of these components of creativity. Fluency refers to the ability of an individual to benefit in a developing situation. This ability helps in using each step completed as a new point where the individual can assess the problem and look forward. Fluency, thus, lays emphasis on the rate of production of all units within all classes. Four varieties of fluencies have been noted: ideational, expressional, associational and word fluency.

(1) *Ideational Fluency*

It is the generation or production of ideas where free expression is encouraged and where quality is not evaluated. These ideas may be generated in terms of words, titles, responses, phrases, sentences, uses, consequences in verbal forms; and in non-verbal forms, drawings, pictures, designs, etc. The idea may be simple as single word and as complex, having a phrase or short sentence or story of unitary thought. When the specifications of the stimulus are known to the person, he can give pertinent possibilities rapidly. Various tests for ideational fluency have been devised to explore headings, improvements, uses, descriptions, topics, themes, things, categories, etc.

(2) *Expressional Fluency*

This type of fluency indicates production of new ideas to fit a system or logical theories. The ideas can be in the form of sentences, question, responses, etc. Tests to measure expressional fluency have been developed to show it directly or through other modes. For example simile interpretations, words arrangements, etc.

(3) *Associational Fluency*

It indicates production of ideas or words from a restricted area, i.e. of equal relationships. It requires completion of relations, like production of relations, generation of synonyms, analogies, similarities, problems of likeness, etc. Some tests measure associational fluency through 'controlled association', 'simile insertions' and 'opposites'.

(4) *Word Fluency*

This fluency requires simply dealing with words. It is generation of words of specifically required epithets. The expressional fluency is concerned only with ideas and sentences whereas word fluency is concerned only with words. Thus, it is more a test of vocabulary. Various tests to measure word fluency use prefix, suffix or first or last letter of words.

Flexibility

Flexibility as used in the interpretation of subject's responses on the test of divergent thinking, represents number of the units of objects. It is indicative of the individual's ability to respond to a stimulus situation. Thus, it can be taken as a measure of variety of response. It indicates in how many distinct different ways an individual can respond to a stimulus. Quantitatively it is a measure of variety. Thus, the number of different classes of ideas or things determines numerical value of flexibility. It differs from fluency in the way that the former is the representation of classes whereas latter is that of units. In case of 'Uses Test', for example, one may give uses of bricks as 'build a house', 'build a school', 'build a factory', etc. Mere fluency is '3' but flexibility is only '1' as the answers belong to only one category of thought. If the answers were 'make a paper-weight', 'drive a nail', 'throw at dog', 'make powder', the flexibility would have been '4', as each new response changed a class.

Originality

Originality refers to the quality of response which reflects the unique and the novel character of product or solution. Hence, the original responses are considered to be uncommon, unusual and infrequent which point toward the individual's attempt to deviate from the mainstream of thought. Various names like, new, uncommon, unusual, singular, individual, idiographic, non-classifiable, novel, unique, remote, infrequent, surprise, etc. are used to designate original response. When the term originality is referred to in terms of either figural or verbal or symbolic transformations, it is designated as uncommon or unusual. When originality is designated statistically, it is named as infrequent, when more concern is shown with the individual or creator. Terms like 'far-fetched', 'novel', and 'different' are employed to designate originality of responses. Thus, it is marked that meaning of originality has been judged from various angles. However, its main criterion is to be away from the main track, or deviation from the accepted path.

Though every test of creativity is scored for originality, yet some specific tests have been developed, where the subject is instructed to produce new ideas, as in plot titles, symbol production, consequences, etc.

Elaboration

It is also an important component of divergent ideas which reflects the expanding and combining activities of higher thought processess. Through elaboration details are specified resulting in the development of general idea. In this way, elaboration makes production of detailed steps, variety of implications and consequences which may be measured quantitatively. Elaboration may be drawn by the 'divergent production' process using 'figural', 'symbolic' and 'semantic' contents to give the product of 'implications'. The use of contents designates or employs the elaboration as figural, symbolic or semantic, etc.

Elaboration may be used for both verbal and non-verbal products as through planning, figure production. Few more important factors have also been taken into account by Guilford and by other research workers. These factors are sensitivity to problems, redefinition, curiosity, etc. but these are not the parts of the Guilford's SI Model.

Sensitivity is the receptivity for problems when the creator observes defects, needs, deficiencies, unusualities and perceives what must be done. Whether the problem is simple or complex he attacks it from various angles.

Redefinition

Redefinition is close to adaptive flexibility and originality and it arises from transformation, specially of convergent productions. It requires defining or perceiving the problem in a way different from the usual, established or intended way, use, etc. It is the ability to re-arrange ideas, concepts, people and things—to shift the function of objects and use them in new ways. It requires imaginative use of old things or ideas for new purposes. It can be applied for different types of contents in the same ways as figural, symbolic, semantic, etc. and they can be named with their names as figural-redefinition, symbolic-redefinition, etc.

Various tests for measuring elaboration have been developed. Some of them are: Figural tests, Symbolic Tests, Semantic Tests including Gestalt Transformations Objective Synthesis, Picture Gestalt.

Curiosity

Curiosity is the root of all knowledge. It is the potential to ask question. Murphy (1958) defined it as the 'tendency to investigate any novelty perceived, tendency to seek information about anything'. He considered it as instinctive as it is the function of sense organs and nervous system, which is more or less inherited by each individual. It includes the stimuli, stimulating sense organs and nervous system, the pursuit the individual makes to know the stimuli, and the persistence that one uses. Murphy regarded that it is first non-specific, as animals and children all poke noses for which they are not concerned; it becomes specific later on when the problem is of great concern and significance. Ausubel (1958) also regarded it so, as the mental and language developments are necessary, because 'why' and 'how' questions are later developments, which are necessary for curiosity. A child rather an infant is incapable of showing curiosity, as he cannot ask question. Empirical evidence also shows that creativity and curiosity are highly related and a high level of curiosity is necessary for creativitv (Day, 1968).

Criticism of 'Guilford's Model of the Structure of Intellect'

Guilford's model of the structure of 'Intellect' is, however, not free from criticisms. The main criticism of Guilford's Model has been that it fails to take into account the existence of general factors running through diverse tests and of group factors which are intermediate in range between the general factor and the host of specific factors. Model of intellect based on hierarchy, as suggested by Burt and Verma (1950, cf. Sharma, K. N., 1979), serves solution to the probelm, as they provide many flexible features. On account of the absence of general factors in the SI Model, Eysenck (1967) called it as 'Hamlet without the Dane'. It cannot be said confidently that no single factor works in all the abilities. For example, memory is such a factor which helps in all cognitions.

Butcher, J. (1970) has cast some doubt on Guilford's distinction of divergent and convergent thinking. He states that it has not been demonstrated so conclusively as many suppose that tests of divergent thinking are properly describable as test of creativity. There is some evidence that scientists are better at convergent thinking and arts specialists at divergent thinking and that, quite apart from this distinction, either kind of specialist may in his own way be 'creative'. Eysenck (1967) extended support to this view and suggested that the divergent thinking of arts specialists largely consists of verbal fluency and is associated with extraversion.

Hudson (1960), in a lively and provocative book, has maintained that the distinction between divergent and convergent thinking is fundamental one, but that is hardly related to creative ability. In his view it is much more closely related to the differences between scientists and specialists in arts or literary subjects. His work with English Public School and Grammar School boys showed a close connection between specialization in arts subjects and divergent thinking and between work in scientific subjects and convergent thinking. Hudson argues this case persuasively, but the selected nature of the sample of subjects with which he worked makes it uncertain how far his results are generalizable. It is very possible that the degree of specialization in the upper forms of selective English schools was the cause rather than the result of the marked distinction in modes of thought. His works clearly merit replication in other kinds of school and at other levels of ability. Cameron (1967) has found partial confirmation of Hudson's views in a study of Aberdeen University undergraduates.

Varela (1969) has proposed that squashing Guilford's cub into a doughnut might do more justice to the generality of intellectual performance across tests. Thus, we see that limiting the number of abilities to only 120 is also arbitrary. It bears no logical basis, except providing a new model with three dimensions of limited number of abilities. He has neither accounted for the abilities falling outside the arena of three dimensions, chosen by him, nor in between them. His model does not provide grounds for the interactions of the processes and their product.

In spite of the various criticisms levelled against Guilford's model of structure of intellect, it cannot be denied that Guilford took a bold step and his attempt and efforts cannot be discredited.

The above detailed note on the divergent thinking process can be of much help to the reader in analysing the measures of creativity which have been generally considered to be akin to the measures of divergent thought process. Hence, the contribution of Guilford has given a new direction to a scientific understanding of creativity.

Before we examine a comprehensive definition of creativity, it is proper to refer to the another aspect of the studies on creativity which emphasizes that individuals roughly fall into two major categories: 'conformers' and the 'creators'. The former group tries to conform to the expectations of others by adopting the prevailing thought and ideas whereas the latter contributes some original ideas and viewpoints and sometime the new product. The creators introduced new mode of perceiving the problems and attacking them. Such individuals are not very much guided by the prescribed norms, rules, or behaviour patterns and thus sometime they become deviant. If one examines creativity in the light of above categorization he will find that an individual is either 'creative' or 'non-creative'. There is no consideration for variation in the degree of creative achievements. However, this notion has little support because it is difficult to divide people into the categories of creative and non-creative as it is difficult to have accurate measures of creativity. Individuals possess varying degree of creative potentials. An individual may be considered as conformer but at the same time he may display some creative art.

Sometimes creativity has been treated to be synonymous with fantasy and imagination. Goldner (1962) holds that creativity is to be considered as an organized, comprehensive, imaginative activity involved in bringing something original. This clearly supports the notion that creative activity lies in innovation rather than reproduction.

Another notion about creativity is that the higher the intelligence, the higher the creativity. Genius is generally considered to be creative. This notion is also wrong as it has been empirically found that minimal level of intelligence is of course required for creative work but it is synonymous with creativity is not admissible. There is little evidence that creativity goes along with higher intelligence. There are various factors which affect creativity. Those who have viewed creativity as inherent ingenious attach little importance to acquisition or environmental stimulation. But this notion is also misleading. Drevdahl (1956) has empirically examined the relationship between intelligence and creativity and found that for the purpose of being creative an individual must have the acquisition of knowledge before it can be used in a novel and original fashion. The relationship between intelligence and creativity has thus been examined from two different angles which needs a thorough discussion citing empirical rasearches. Hence, the reader will again come across this discussion in the following chapter.

Considering the multi-dimensional nature of creativity Rhodes (1961) analysed fifty definitions of creativity and indicated four strands of creativity: person, process, product, and press. The definitions stressing a cluster of related personality traits and mental ability of the person to create something new fall into the category of 'persons'. The definitions which ignore creativity being cluster of personality traits or mental qualities for searching, combining and synthesizing and lay emphasis on creativity as a process, fall in the category of 'process'. Such definitions attach much importance to the functioning in the mind of the creatives. The category of product includes such definitions of creativity which emphasize the 'outcome' or the 'product' being original, unique, valuable and novel. The last category of 'press' includes the views of such psychologists who emphasize the significant role of favourable external and internal environment of the individual for creative output. A detailed discussion on these four major categories is as follows:

Persons

Simpson (1922) considered cognitive structure in creative ability as the initiative which is manifested in an altogether different pattern of thought regarding problems of identification. The creative individual has distinct mental qualities for searching, combing and synthesizing. The creative potentials are further recognized in terms of curiosity, imagination, discovery and innovation. Wallac (1926) also recognized abilities for creating a problem and then originating and inventing an idea or concept and finally preparing a cognitive picture along a new dimension. Guilford (1950) has also laid emphasis on 'ability gradient' and stressed its divergent characteristics. He has clearly introduced the individual's ability of generation of information derived from giving information in his model of structure of intellect. He talked of innovation, originality and typical synthesis present in the creative person.

Getzels and Jackson (1962) have also considered creativity as a specific type of cognitive ability which has its reflexion in the performance of the subjects on verbal test of creativity. Creativity, he claims, depends upon novel and varied responses on the test task. Bowenfeld (1952) also recognized eight significant characteristics of a creative individual. The characteristics were, sensitivity, fluency, flexibility, originality, redefinition, abstracting, synthesizing and organizing capabilities of the individual. Torrance (1962) in his pioneer work in the field of creativity picked up eighty-four important qualities of creatives. Many other experts in this field have recognized a number of personality traits and specific mental abilities which contribute to creative activities. It seems sufficient to remark on the basis of review of literature that the personality of creatives differs from that of non-creatives in many ways. A separate chapter has been also devoted on this issue in the present book.

Creativity as Process

Spearman (1930) considered creative thinking as the process of visualizing or creating relationships with both conscious or sub-conscious processes operating. Barchillon (1961) took a broader view of creativity as process. Spearman emphasized simply mental functioning whereas he considered thinking process in two different kinds: 'Cognito', meaning to take and throw things together and 'Intelligo', that is, to choose and discriminate from many alternative possibilities and then synthesizing the element in a novel and original way. Guilford also believed in the process when he clearly defined the divergent thinking as the process of forming the hypothesis, testing it and finally communicating the result. Torrance (1965) examined creativity as a process through which a creative individual manifests sensitivity to the problems, deficiencies, missing elements and irregularities. He is very much anxious for the correct identification of the problem and its solution by way of formulating hypotheses about deficiencies, testing and re-testing it in the light of various modifications and ultimately achieves solution of the problem. Chiseline (1952) treats creativity as a process of change, development and evaluation and finally the organization. Yamamoto (1964) also defined creativity as a process by which new ideas or hypotheses are formed, tested and finally results are communicated. Taylor (1955); Rhodes (1961); John Dewey (1910) ; and Rossman (1931) also considered creativity in terms of process. Rossman (1931) stated that an inventor has to pass through seven steps in the process of creativity; a need or difficulty is observed; the problem is formulated; information in hand is surveyed; solutions are formulated; and then critically examined; new ideas are formulated and finally these ideas are tested. However, Vinacke (1960) observed that creative thinking is necessarily to be conceived in terms of dynamic and inter-playing activities rather than as discrete stages. Mackinnon (1960) has advanced the concept of creativity as a time dimension processes involving originality, realization and adoptiveness. Thus, in spite of subtle differences among the opinions the above note on creativity emphasizes creativity as a process.

Creativity and Press

Press may be considered as the interaction between persons and their environment. Persons emphasizing the importance of press observed that it is the environmental effect that motivates an individual for pursuing certain creative activities. Maslow was the pioneer in defining creativity in terms of press.

Vinacke (1960) while defining creativity emphasized the integrated harmony between external reality and internalized needs of the individual. The creative potentials may be present within the individual but for its proper expression and reflexion a rich and stimulating environment is needed. The environment must provide an opportunity to the individuals for the outlet of hidden potentials. Stephens (1954) has stressed the importance of family life on the growth of creativity. The parents may provide a healthy environment by way of stimulating the children. The atmosphere must be challenging. Beside home environment the school environment plays also significant role in fostering creativity. In school the individual enters into a competitive environment from protective one at home. The school conditions, teacher-pupil relationship, and intellectual, satisfying congenial atmosphere in the school have been found to affect the development of creativity in a satisfying manner (Moore, 1961; Ward *et al.* 1970; Johnson, 1973; Glover, 1973 and Worthen, 1968), while dealing with the environmental and familial factors behind creative growth one has to consider the socio-economic condition of the family which provides resources and opportunities for the expression of hidden creative potentials. Earl (1973); Khataea (1971); Gupta *et al.* 1976; Agrawal *et al.* 1977; Singh, 1978; Srivastava, 1978; Sharma, 1980 have emphasized the role of better socio-economic status in fostering the growth of creative components. However, caution is to be taken while generalizing the domineering influence of environmental variables on creativity. There are many other factors which contribute to creative activities. However, this much seems convincing that 'press' has distinct role to play in creative work.

Creativity and Product

The creativity is represented in terms of novel and original products. Rhodes, while defining creativity, considered products as the major strand of it. While dealing with the product in relation to creativity one treats the former as the real measure of creativity. Guilford's pioneer work in the area of creativity measurement, in a highly systematic way, stressed divergent thought production as the real creative output. These were generation of information from given information where the variety of output from the same source has been emphasized. On the basis of factor analytical studies of the indicators of creativity, Guilford suggested fluency, flexibility and originality as measurable units. However, one must take into consideration the other influencing agents while accepting product or the outcome as the measuring yard of creativity.

The foregoing note on four strands of creativity (person, process, press and product) is suggestive of the fact that they have independent places in the area of creativity. Sharma, K.N. (1979) has presented a detailed account of these four aspects of creative thinking. The present author feels that these four should not be considered as contradiction to each other rather as supplement to each other. The overall picture of creativity can be better presented if a holistic viewpoint is adopted. What is needed is to adopt a flexible approach and to mingle up these four aspects in such a scientific way that each of them maintains its identity in spite of the pressure from other. The way in which these four strands have been examined seems to be confusing. Where is the harm if we fundamentally analyze creativity as a process first then proceed to observe it concretely in terms of objective unit of measurement or product and further we incorporate the idea that there are certain personal characteristics which may be reflective of the creative potentials to an extent and finally some weightage is given to the stimulating and harmonious environmental conditions in which creativity can have its full expression. In short, 'person', 'process', 'product' and 'press' should be considered as a combined and larger unit of the study of creativity.

Before we shift to other related aspects of creativity it seems proper to make the readers acquainted with the views of Freud, Alfred Adler, Abraham, and Maslow. These three prominent psychologists have their distinct and original contribution toward the analysis of creative behaviour. The inclusion of these three viewpoints also suggests the importance of creativity as a subjects for study even by great pioneers of psychology.

Regarding creativity Freud has pointed out that the development of civilization was made possible by the inhibition of primitive object—choices and the diversion of instinctual energy into socially acceptable and culturally creative channels. A displacement that produces a higher cultural achievement is called a sublimation. Freud observed in this connection that Leonardo da Vinci's interest in painting Madonnas was a sublimated expression of a longing for intimacy with his mother from whom he had been separated at a tender age. This sublimation, as a defence is adopted by the ego to fulfil those socially disapproved and threatening impulses which were repressed into the unconscious. By sublimation the unconscious motives get their expression through socially approved channels. The painter through his painting, the poet through his poem take help of such channels of expression which are socially and culturally approved. Creative works thus, can be the product of the sublimated tendencies. Hence, Freud very much emphasized the role of unconscious desires behind creation. Hogan, R. (1966) holds that according to Freud artistic creations are neurotic symptoms made public: each work of art reflects more or less directly the artist's unconscious. Freud did feel, however, that the more sophisticated the artist, the more complex were his creations and the more disguised were the unconscious trends. Freud claims that the sublimation or sexual instincts serve as the prime instigator for great advances in western culture and knowledge. He argued that the sublimation of sexual motives is an especially conspicuous feature of cultural revolution; sublimation alone makes it possible for this zealous scientific and artistic activities which play so important a part in our civilized life.

When Adler—a great adherent of Freud—discovered the creative power of the self all other concepts were subordinated to it. The unitary, consistent, creative self, sovereign in the personality structure. The doctrine of a 'creative self' asserts that human beings make their own personalities. They construct them out of the raw material of heredity and experience.

While taking into account the Adler's concept of inferiority feelings and compensation, one can also analyse creativity in different manners. Adler very much emphasized the feeling of inferiority within the individual which is universal. The individual makes attempt at compensating this feeling either by going into the world of fantasy or neurosis or sometimes compensating it in a highly positive and creative manner. The creative work of an individual may represent his basic urge for compensation and achievement. The individual's effort toward achieving perfection may result in creative work.

The primacy of human creativity is perhaps the most significant concept of humanistic psychology. Maslow (1950) merits the distinction of being the first to call attention to the fact that the most universal characteristics of all the people he studied or observed was their creativeness. Describing it as fundamental characteristics common to human nature Maslow (1970) viewed creativity as a potentiality present in all people at birth. Maslow argued: It is natural that trees sprout leaves, birds fly, humans create. However, Maslow also recognized that most human beings loose it as they become unculturated (formal education stains out a lot of it). Happily some few individuals hold on to this fresh, naive and direct way of looking at things or if they number among the majority who loose it, they are able to recover it later in life. Maslow theorizes that since creativity is potential in any one, it requires no special talents or capacities. One need not write books, compose music or produce art objects to be creative. Comparatively few people do. Creativity is an universal human function and leads to all forms of self expression. Maslow found that without exception creativity was more prominent in self actualizers than in any other. The kind of self actualizing creativity appears in everyday life as an expression of a personality which is perceptive, spontaneous and childlike. Basically it revolves around the discovery of things new and novel that depart from conventional ideas.

Thus, it becomes clear that the analysis of creativity has been made in multiple direction. The popular meaning has given birth to the scientific definition of creativity. However, even today after the introduction of Guilford model of intellect it seems difficult to develop a highly scientific and concrete idea of creativity. Even Guilford has been criticized by other investigators. Further, it may be mentioned that some of the definitions may be acceptable to the researchers but they are also not complete as they fail to cover all the important elements required even for a workable definition. Amidst these controversies Hurlock (1978) has selected the definition given by Drevdahl (1964) which may be considered to be a good and workable definition. He has considered creativity as the capacity of individuals to produce compositions, products or ideas of any sort which are essentially novel and of which the individual was not aware before. Further he states that creativity may be considered as an imaginative activity where one finds synthesis of thoughts. Through this activity the information derived from past experiences are synthesized and treated in the light of new patterns and combinations which results in generation of new correlates. Further, it has been pointed out that creative activites must follow a purpose or goal and not to be guided by fantasy. It is not essential that creative work may have immediate practical application or be a perfect or complete product. It may further take the form of artistic, literary or scientific creation or simply it may be of methodological character. Thus, Drevdahl has covered many aspects of creativity and emphasized its complex nature.

Further, at this point of concluding remarks regarding creativity as a concept, the author wants to emphasize that mostly creativity has been taken to be a process which is a goal directed either in context of personal benefit or that of the group. This activity culminates in producing something novel or different. Creativity may have its root in divergent thinking process which brings diversified responses on the measures of creativity. This ability to create something new utilizes the available information and knowledge. Creativity may be taken in the form of controlled imagination that results in the achievement of some kind.

Sharma (1979) has also quoted the important criteria of creativity which are based on proposition of Hallman (1963); Jackson (1965); and Mednick (1969). These criteria include connectedness, originality, non-rationality, self-actualization and openness. Connectedness involves the application of relationship between existing elements. The newly created connections should not be taken to be equivalent to the different parts which are connected. The characteristic feature of this relationship among the parts is metaphoric and transformational. This connectedness has been synonymously used with combination, new organization, synthesis, integration or meaningful fusion, etc. Bruner (1962) emphasized that creativity grows out of an individual's effort to place the existing objects in a quite new perspective. Arnold (1959) and Ghiselin (1952) have considered creativity as the combination of past experiences into new patterns or configuration which is satisfying to the creator and the society. Murrey (1959) has also emphasized the compositional process resulting in some novel object, experience or image. The common agreement, thus, seems among many writers regarding combining or recombining the elements into new relations or patterns for which efforts are needed by the creator.

As far as originality is concerned it has been already noted earlier that novelty or uniqueness of the creative output has been well recognized by majority of investigators. Hallmann (1963) has given four characteristic features of originality which are novelty, unpredictability, uniqueness and surprise. References to original ideas have been also made by using words like remoteness of associations and uncommonness of responses.

However, the common notion that what is created is always new and different from what already existed and, therefore, it is unique, is also not very much acceptable nowadays. Originality or exploration may better be analyzed in the light of framing of new combination. Barron (1975) has argued that creativity does not mean only exploring, inventing or discovering new things or relations rather it means to make new combination from already existing objects and elements. However, amidst such criticisms it has been observed that a number of investigators still stress that the creator produces something new, different and original.

Non-rationality as one of the criteria of creativity: The creative work of an individual has been explained on the basis of various mental processes which produce new connections. It is non-rational because the activities responsible for this combinations take place in the form of unconscious operation. It has been argued that in individual's effort at creating something new is not based on conscious rationalization as creation resists rational analysis and lies below the surface of consciousness. The stages of incubation and illumination in creative thinking extend support to the above connotation. After the stage of preparation the individual while in rest and upwardly being detached from the problem finds the solution and thus illumination is perceived. The period of incubation has been referred to as individual's unconscious involvements with the problem. It does not mean that creativity is not the result of an individual's conscious efforts, as it also plays its role in the analysis of the situation and its elaborating and testing aspects.

Self-actualization has been referred to as a criterion of creativity. On this concept Maslow's and that of Goldstem's opinion are worth quoting, who claim that an individual strives continuously to realize his inherent potentialities by whatever avenues are open. This singleness of purpose gives directive and unity to one's life. The primacy of human creativity is perhaps the most significant concept of humanistic psychology. Maslow characterizes self-actualization as the desire to become everything that one is capable of becoming. Self-actualization is a person's desire for self-improvement, his or her drive to make actual what he or she is potentially. In short, to self-actualize is to become the kind of person one wants to become—to reach the peak of one's potential: 'a musician must compose music, an artist must paint, a poet must write, if he is to be at peace with himself.' However, Maslow has also argued that self-actualization need not take the form of creative and artistic endeavour. An athlete, a student or teacher or an ardent labourer may all be actualizing their potentials in doing well what each does the best. Specific forms of self-actualization vary greatly from person to person. However, not surprisingly, Maslow found out that without exception, creativity was more prominent in self-actualizers than in others. Basically, it revolves around the discovery of things new and novel that depart from conventional ideas. He believes that when self-actualization touches special talent it calls for creativeness. The self-actualizing personality is characterized by an unusually strong motivational drive which energizes the individual in a way he is compelled to act, to express, to perform and produce personality transformations. On the whole Maslow's approach to creativity, on the basis of the self-actualization motive, stimulated many others to explain creative activities generated by the presence of some motives of one or another kind within the individual. In short, it can be said that self-actualization has been also considered as one of the criteria of creativity.

Appropriateness

Appropriateness, as a criterion of creativity, is associated with the assessment of the nature and quality of the creative output. It is generally applied in creativity testing. While judging creativity against this criterion one expects that the product of creativity must make sense in the light of the situational demands and the specifications of the producer. The appropriateness may be judged in terms of satisfaction and appropriateness as well as accuracy. However, a product to be accurate and perfect does not need 100% accuracy or perfection. While analyzing the response of the respondents on the test of creativity in terms of appropriateness the observer is guided by the set standards formulated by the person who has developed the test for judging the responses on the items. Appropriateness, as a criterion of creativity, helps in eliminating the absurd responses. The criterion of appropriateness is associated with the principle of fitness. It may have a logical base. Appropriateness should be considered as a continuous one and is to be judged in terms of degree.

Usefulness is also an important criterion of creative product. Mednick (1962) while introducing this criterion of creativity argued that a response to be useful must be creative. He stressed the inclusion of this criterion because he realized that unusualness or originality are not sufficient to explain creative activities.

'Transformation' as a criterion of creativity has been also

emphasized. The creative product has the quality to transform the constraints of reality. Some products combine elements which are not befitting to tradition as they have been presented in new perspective. They compel the observer to perceive reality in new ways. Jackson and Massick (1965) referred to transformation as a process which involves a radical change in the existing approach to a subject or in handling the material. Thus, transformation makes the product deviating from the prescribed norm. This changes the perceiver's conventional mode of perceiving or thinking about his world.

'Condensation' has been also referred to as the criterion against which a product can be judged to be creative. Condensation involves unity and coherence of meaning. It involves the ordered arrangement of the contents in a way which can be interpreted in many ways by observers. Various elements are presented in such an organized way within a limited range that it has its own form.

Openness refers to acceptance of things and ideas in a way which lacks rigidity and stereotyped beliefs, perceptions and hypotheses. It includes characteristics like sensitivity, tolerance for ambiguity, self-acceptance and spontaneity. Sensitivity refers to awareness of things as they are rather than by predetermined set. The creative individual is sensitive to the objects, ideas, problems and gaps. Fromm, 1959; Guilford, 1957; Stein, 1960 and others considered sensitivity to be quite significant for creative output. Tolerance for ambiguity characterizes an individual to accept conflict and tension, as well as inconsistencies, contradictions and further to be comfortable amidst ambiguous and vague issues.

'Spontaneity' helps an individual in becoming free and autonomous in approach. On the whole, it can be remarked that openness involving sensitivity, tolerance for ambiguity, spontaneity and acceptance of self facilitates creative performance as it takes the creator away from stereotyped behaviour pattern, and set rules of conduct and predetermined belief system and action tendencies.

The above note on various criteria of creativity does not

restrict other qualities or characteristics of a creative product, various other criteria have also been set by other investigators.

The above note on creativity indicates that investigation of creativity received considerable impetus from the growing demand for research and screening of talented individuals so that better guidance could be given to them from the early stage. Studies of scientific talent have become increasingly concerned with creative abilities. Creativity has been regarded as the primary quality in artistic production and also as a basis for scientific production.

Investigation of variables associated with creative achievement have followed different approaches. Some investigators have concentrated on the creator's biographial history and antecedent experiences, others have investigated into the situational variables which favour creative expression. Some researchers have made extensive clinical study of the highly eminent scientists whereas others have used psychometric tools and observational procedures for assessing creative talents in the light of specific personality characteristics. However, in general, tests of divergent thinking have been developed and used for measuring creativity. The respondents' scores on verbal and non-verbal items are analyzed for measuring creative potentials. The screening of creativity on the basis of psychological test is in greater use because of objectivity and ease. With this purpose in mind various tests have been developed abroad and also in India.

Some of the widely used tests of creativity in foreign countries are those of Torrance, Guilford and Wallach and Kogan. In India also various tests of creativity have been either developed or adapted in Hindi to suit our Hindi speaking population. The tests developed/adapted by Mehdi B (1973) (Appendix-I), Paramesh (1969) and Sharma (1964) in our country have been widely used for measuring creativity. The tests of creativity generally measure subject's responses on the test items in the context of fluency, flexibility, elaboration and originality.

'Sex difference' as a variable in Creativity

While going through the conceptual and empirical views regarding sex difference in creativity, the author observed that these views are still controvercial. Some studies have shown the superiority of males over females and some of females over the males on test of creativity. Further, there are studies which have reported non-significant differences between the members of the two sexes with regard to their creative performance. This suggests that sex and creativity are independent of each other. In the light of such studies it is difficult to have an agreed opinion regarding role of 'sex difference' in creativity. Some of the important studies available in this area are as follows.

Kelley (1965) studied creativity of a sample of fourth grade male and female students and found that boys were significantly more creative than girl respondents on the measures of non-verbal creativity. The study of Strauss and Strauss (1968) on a cross-cultural population has also indicated a significant sex difference in American and Indian population. The male respondents were found to be significantly higher creatives in comparison to their female counterparts. Further, the wider gaps were explored among Indian subjects than American. The researcher attributed this gap among male and female respondents to the degree of cultural and social advancement in America. During the period of this study in India, the females were far behind in many respects than the males. The females were less exposed to education, socio-cultural advancement, training devices, imaginative endeavour and mass-media communication which might have blocked the expression and growth of their creative potentials.

In another study, conducted by Prakash (1966), on a fourth grade Indian children, the boys were found to be significantly higher on creativity as compared to the girls. Raina (1971) has also shown the boys to be superior to the girls in respect of their creative performance. However, he has taken into account the restrictions on girls imposed by the family and society at large, as the factor behind their inferior performance as compared to their male counterparts. Gagneja (1972) has also studied the superiority of boys over girls with regard to creativity.

MAR 'L, S.K. (1971) studied a sample of eighth grade Arab rural subjects and observed that male subjects obtained higher scores on Torrance test of creative thinking as compared to female respondents.

Torrance (1962, 1965); Torrance and Aliotti (1969) in their study on US sample found male respondents to be significantly higher on the measures of verbal originality.

Dhir (1973) found boys to be superior on figural originality. Guilford (1964) and Harlow (1967) have also reported male subjects to be superior on semantic flexibility and total flexibility respectively.

Middents (1968) in a study on 191 female and 123 male samples found that the latter scored significantly higher on the test of creativity (non-verbal elaboration) as compared to girls.

Kogan (1974) surveying the literature on sex differences has aptly remarked that the greater susceptibility of women to distraction related to social context handicaps their creative achievements.

Hussain, S. (1985) in his study on tribal and non-tribal male and female students found boys to be superior to their female counterparts on different aspects of creativity.

In a recent study on Indian population (N = male 200 and female 200), Sajid, S.M. in collaboration with Hussain, S. (1984) compared the mean scores of male and female respondents on verbal and non-verbal test of creativity (composite scores as well as scores on various components). The findings suggested that the female respondents had higher scores on verbal creativity (composite mean scores as well as scores on fluency, flexibility, and originality) as compared to male subjects. The differences were also significant at .01 level of confidence. The two groups were also compared on intelligence and socio-economic status.

However, the male respondents were found to be better on 'originality' aspect of non-verbal creativity as well as on its composite scores. The differences between the mean scores of male and female were significiant at .01 level of confidence.

As far as the elaboration aspect on non-verbal creativity is concerned the difference between the mean scores of male and female respondents was not found to be statistically significant.

However, upwardly females appeared to have a greater mean score as compared to males. The statistical results in detail are presented in the table 1.1.

A significant aspect of the above study is that while comparing male and female respondents on creativity the investigator also measured their intelligence as he himself found in his study that intelligence might contribute to creativity upto certain level. This gave more strength to the findings with regard to sex difference in creativity. However, in the above study the male and female respondents did not differ significantly on intelligence mean scores (111.42 and 109.54 $P<.05$). So there was greater probability of other factors generating the difference in creativity scores of male and female groups. Another thing which is to be remarked in this direction is that perhaps this is the first extensive study on Indian population indicating, on the whole, superiority of female over males because in previous studies usually the results are in favour of males. Hence, this needs further arguments. The present author while going through other details of the study observed that female respondents scored higher mean scores on socio-economic status scale as compared to their male counterparts, and the difference was significant (55.05 and 48.04 respectively $P<.01$). This analysis of boys and girls with regard to their SES is suggestive of the fact that higher SES might have contributed to the better performance of females on the test of verbal and non-verbal creativity. The positive contribution of higher SES to creative growth has been already supported by Sajid, S.M. (1984) and many other investigators.

The females are now more exposed to educational facilities. There is lesser imposition of restrictions on them by the society and culture. They are now very much inspired and encouraged for creative work. The attitude towards them is now a bit more liberal. They do not feel very much handicapped and discouraged as they experienced in past.

During the last 10 to 15 years there has been tremendous change in the attitude of the society toward girls. Somewhat liberal treatment is being given to the girls at large. Now they are more exposed to the outer world. Specially the urban population is having greater educational facilities, training and

TABLE 1.1

Mean Scores of Male and Female Respondents (N=200 each) on IB Scores, SES as well as on Separate Components of Verbal and non-Verbal Creativity along with Composite Scores

			Verbal				*Non-verbal*		
	IB	*SES*	*Fluency*	*Flex*	*Orig.*	*Verbal Flu.+ Flex.+Orig. composite*	*Elab.*	*Orig.*	*Non-verbal Elab.+Orig. composite*
Male (N=200)									
Mean	111.425	48.04	34.58	23.52	14.21	72.31	71.51	30.77	102.28
SD	12.95	9.60	11.59	7.94	7.06	23.21	18.82	23.90	42.72
Female (N=200)									
Mean	109.54	55.05	37.80	27.03	18.20	83.03	73.56	17.63	91.19
SD	18.98	7.62	9.09	7.37	9.04	25.50	18.19	13.12	31.31
't'	1.16	8.06	3.09	4.57	4.92	4.79	1.10	6.81	3.56
	N.S.	P<.01	P<.01	P<.01	P<.01	P<.01	P<.05	P<.01	P<.01
N	398	398	398	398	398	398	398	398	398

enjoying greater social interactions. The girls have entered into the competitive world. Naturally the restrictions imposed by sociocultural background are less as compared to previous ones. Hence, it is not surprising that females can compete with males even on creative performance. The author further feels that in our society now the hidden potentialities of women's population are much more cared for and opportunities are also provided for their growth and development, specially in families belonging to a high socio-economic status group. In the light of these considerations the empirical findings of Sajid, S.M. (1984) can be well substantiated.

The findings of Sajid, S.M. can also be supported by other studies. Yamamoto (1960) found girls to be higher on creativity than boys though the boys had higher IQ scores. This supports that girls can surpass boys on creativity and further shows the independent functions of intelligence and creativity in both the sexes.

Neufeld, 1964; Dauw, 1966; and Fletcher, 1968 have also studied the high school male and female students in respect of their creative thinking abilities and found the girl population to have an edge over boys.

Razik (1964) and Bowers (1971) studied college students and found that females outranked the males in their creativity. Goyal (1973) conducted study on the sample of teachers training college and found that girls exhibited superior performance on verbal fluency and flexibility than boys as measured with Torrance test of creative thinking.

Hussain and Hussain (1975) in their study on male and female samples using tests of novel uses, consequences and unusual uses and elaboration found significant differences in favour of girls on unusual uses test (originality measures) whereas on other three tests the differences were not significant though the girls had higher mean scores on all these tests.

Cacha (1971) studied fifth grade children and Burgees (1971) studied elementary students and the two investigators reported girls to be superior to boys on certain measures of creativity. Thus these Indian studies extend support to the findings of Sajid, S.M.

(1984), which indicated overall superiority of girl students to their boys counterparts.

The above detailed note on creative performance, attributed to sex differences, leaves one still in a state of uncertainty. It seems difficult to remark whether males are superior to females or vice versa. The studies quoted above support this argument of the author. No doubt this much can be accepted that sex difference contributes to differences in creativity. However, as far as the relative position of male and female subjects on test of creativity is concerned, the problem of generalization arises. Some studies have indicated males to be superior whereas others females to be superior. This in itself reflects the role of some other factors affecting the performance of male and female on test of creativity. The socio-cultural stimulation and advancement, SES, incentives for growth and development in home and school and college environment, availability of resources for creative output, personality characteristics and other such factors may be considered in this context. Thus, sex in itself should not be treated in isolation, as a factor in creative pursuit. Studies should be conducted on various samples controlling all possible cognitive, conative and affective factors and isolating 'sex difference' as a factor in creating difference on creative measures. What is unfortunate is that studies available in this direction have mostly yielded results without greater control on extraneous variables. Now we need an intensive approach to the study of sex difference or other factors which have been associated with creativity. Small samples should be preferred so that maximum control may be exercised and the investigator can well isolate the effect of one variable on creativity.

CHAPTER TWO

INTELLIGENCE AND CREATIVITY

The relationship of intelligence to creativity has been considered to be highly significant, at the same time highly controversial. However, creativity was so much considered in the recent past as an integral component of intelligence that it was not very much considered a separate topic for independent and comprehensive researches. In this connection the remarks of Butcher, H.J. (1970) are worth quoting. He has well remarked in his book *Human Intelligence* (1970) that 15 years ago a book on intelligence would have been unlikely to deal with this subject at all. Creativity was defined by most of the pioneer researchers to be on the fringe of psychology and hardly capable of being investigated by using empirical method. Authors like Galton, Havelock Ellis and Cocks, had written books on estimated intelligence of people, no doubt, but few attempts had been made to investigate into creative abilities and their correlates. The common opinion was that anything which could be described as creativity except at the level of genius, was largely accounted for by the known and measurable abilities. Spearman (1950) ; Burt (1962), and Vernon (1964) held that much of what passes for creativity can be ascribed to general intelligence. However, during the last two decades investigators started questioning the study of creativity in the light of intelligence. There was a conviction that creative abilities could be distinguished from general intelligence both conceptually and in terms of measurement and assessment. The available psychological tests of mental ability were criticized for not measuring creative ability. These tests did not intend to measure creativity as the essential nature of the tests did not permit individualized or unique responses. Further, available psychological tests of mental ability could reveal what levels of intellectual ability are demanded and what levels of particularized abilities (verbal, mathematical, spatial, immediate and remote recall, etc.) are essential in each of the creative fields. Some reported that test of general intelligence might reflect the superior intelligence or gifted general mental capacities, but not everyone who attains this higher level of intelligence, as measured by the test of intelligence, will prove to be creative. People started thinking of non-intellective personality traits and environmental variables behind creative behaviour. Such awakening generated interest in the study of creativity as a separate problem and not only linked with the study of intelligence. A number of articles started appearing on this topic. Parnes & Brunelle (1967) have reported that about 1250 articles had come out in the preceding one-and-half year in America. Cognitive tests in general use were found to be limited and narrow with regard to the ability they measure by using specific types of item. The tests of general intelligence and special abilities and aptitudes were also exposed to such criticisms. It was argued that the kind of material employed and the usual multiple-choice item direct the respondent's thinking along a restricted range if he has to find out the correct response. If the respondent reports an original and justifiable answer which was not considered by the test constructor, he will be adversely judged. The multiple-choice item of a test were enough to exclude original thinking. This idea regarding the minimum chance for expression of original and unique responses as well as personal synthesis in performance on the conventional kind of test very much lowered the significance of intelligence test in measuring creativity. People thought that creative abilities could not be objectively assessed because of its intangible and elusive qualities.

Another line of criticism about the established tests of ability was that they had failed to screen people whose subsequent careers had given proof of exceptional talent. Werthimer (1959) has well quoted the case of Einstein, who was not a bright student at school but proved his exceptional creative talent on his own account. At lower level also Mackenon (1962) has indicated that architects of distinction and persons of other professions having outstanding achievements were reported to be students of just average intelligence. All such references and considerations prepared a ground for assessing creativity not only from intellectual angle but from that of temperamental and motivational field.

Thurstone (1958) emphasized this distinction and provided a provocative analysis of the possible role of ideational fluency, inductive reasoning and certain perceptual tendencies in creative behaviour. He also called special attention to the contribution of non-intellectual, temperamental factors to creative activity. He observed that creativity is encouraged by a receptive as contrasted to a critical attitude toward novel ideas and that creative solutions are more likely to occur during periods of relaxed, dispersed attention than during periods of active concentration on a problem.

Jersild, T. (1978) has also commented as a result of correlational studies of creativity and intelligence among those designated highly creative, that the correlation between the two variables was low but positive. Further, he has quoted Mcnemar (1964) who said that creativity in a given area may require quite different abilities from creativity in another area. Among architects, creativity may reflect the ability to engineer structural innovations, in which case it should be a correlate of intelligence. If the creativity depends on new artistic design, intelligence would probably be less important. The kind of creativity involved, then, may be a factor in the size of correlation to be expected.

Benett (1909) and Thurston (1938), no doubt, recognized the limitations of intelligence test as measuring instrument of creativity but the credit goes to Guilford (1950) who advocated strongly not to equate creativity with intelligence. Guilford, J.P., who introduced the 'structure of intellect' selected creativity as a topic on which his presidential address to the APA was delivered. His distinction between convergent and divergent thought processes, generated much enthusiasm for experimental investigation of creativity in the form of divergent thinking.

The study of Getzels and Jackson (1962) can also be treated as pioneer in which attempts were made to find out differences between 'highly intelligent and highly creative children'. They argued that giftedness in children has been frequently defined as a score on a test of intelligence and typically such studies have been equated with the study of intelligence quotient as a single variable. They put forward various confusions involved in such studies. Firstly, there was the limitation of the single metric itself which not only restricted the investigator's perspective of the more general phenomenon, but placed on the one concept a greater theoretical and predictive burden than it intended to carry. They further ascertained that for all practical purposes the term 'gifted child' has become synonymous with the expression 'child with a high IQ', which makes the observer blind to other forms of excellence. Further, they argued that within the universe of intellectual functions themselves we have most often behaved as if the intelligence tests represented an adequate sampling of all mental abilities and cognitive processes. Despite the already substantial and increasing literature regarding the intellectual functions closely associated with creativity, we still treat the latter concept as acceptable only to performance in one or more of the arts to the exclusion of other types of achievement requiring inventiveness, originality and perfection. The synonymous use of creative child and the artistic talented child has limited one's attempts to identify and foster cognitive abilities related to creative functioning in areas other than the arts. Getzels and Jackson thus ascertained that the use of IQ in defining giftedness reflected the fact that previously the enquiries in this field were made in the classroom context and heavily concerned with academic abilities and achievement. If one starts moving outside the classroom setting, during making enquiries he might identify cognitive characteristics defining giftedness for other situations just as the IQ did in the classroom.

In the course of such studies on creativity, the study conducted by Getzels and Jackson (1962) attracted most attention towards the differences between 'highly intelligent' and 'highly creative children'.

Butcher H.J. (1970) has also traced out the development of the independent and comprehensive researches in the field of creativity and intelligence which could suggest that the former cannot be simply studied as one aspect of intelligence and that the tests of intelligence cannot be taken as the tests of creativity. In other words, scores on intelligence test cannot be the indicative of an individual's creative performance because many non-intellective components play their role in creative performance.

Getzels and Jackson also referred to the issues raised by the American Association for gifted children which favoured the inclusion of qualities other than IQ in conceptualizing giftedness. The gifted individual was defined as a person whose performance in any line of socially useful endeavour is consistently superior. This definition includes individuals having high talent in art, music, drama, and mathematics as well as those who possess mechanical and social skills and also those with high abstract verbal intelligence. Even amidst such conception of a gifted child it has been a practice in research and education to treat IQ metric as an exclusive criterion of giftedness.

Butcher (1970) has remarked that the school studied by Getzels and Jackson was an atypical one, being a private school in which a large proportion of the pupils came from the families of lecturers at the University of Chicago, and only a negligible proportion from the families of semi-skilled or unskilled workers. The mean IQ of the children was 132.

The method adopted was to form two contrasting groups, one of pupils who scored very high on measures of intelligence (even compared with the general level in the school) and relatively low on tests of creativity, and the other of those who scored high on the tests of creativity and relatively low on the tests of intelligence. There were five creativity measures, some of which were taken or adapted from tests made up by Guilford and by Cattell, and others specially constructed by the authors. The five measures were, briefly, as follows:

1. Word association. Meanings and uses required of common words with multiple meanings, e.g., 'bolt', 'sack'; scored both for number of definitions, and number of radically different meanings.

2. Uses for things. As many different uses as possible to be given for objects such as 'brick', 'paper-clip'; scored for number of uses and originality of uses.

3. Hidden shapes (part of Cattell's Objective-Analytic Test Battery). 18 simple geometrical figures, each followed by

four complex figures. Subject required to find the geometric figure hidden in the more complex pattern.

4. Fables. Four fables were presented in which the last lines were missing. The subject was required to provide three different endings to each story, one moralistic, one humorous and one sad.

5. Make-up problems. Four complex paragraphs containing many numerical statements were presented. Subjects required to make up as many mathematical problems as possible from them (but no need to solve them). Scored on number, complexity, appropriateness, and originality of problems.

Correlations between these measures and of each measure with IQ were calculated for 292 boys and 241 girls separately. All correlation coefficients were positive, and of moderate size, between +.1 and +.5, those for the girls being slightly higher. The five separate measures were then combined into one composite measure of creativity, though this is not made clear in the report. At least, performance on these five measures of creativity was one criterion and IQ the other, by which the contrasting groups were formed, one high creativity group (all in top-scoring 20% on creativity, but below top-scoring 20% in IQ) and one high IQ group (vice versa). Because it is not made clear how the five creativity measures were combined into a single criterion; it is also not quite clear in detail how the contrasting groups were formed. They were at any rate reduced in number because some of the subjects were required for other aspects of the study, with the result that out of 533 original subjects, the 'high creativity' group contained 26 and the 'high IQ' group 28 children.

Interesting and important similarities and differences were found by Getzels and Jackson between the 'high creativity' and 'high IQ' groups. Most striking perhaps was the finding that the high creativity group equalled the high IQ groups in scholastic achievement (assessed by a composite score on several standardized tests) in spite of having an average IQ 23 points lower (127 against 150). This result suggests the possibility that some or all of the creativity measures might be used as predictors of scholastic achievement. Getzels and

Jackson, in fact, report quite high positive correlations .3 and .6) between some of the individual tests and both verbal and numerical achievement for the whole sample of 533 subjects. The three tests which showed up best in this way were Word Association, Make-up Problems, and Hidden Shapes in that order. Getzels and Jackson also attempted to find out whether this unexpectedly high degree of scholastic achievement on the part of the high creativity group could be ascribed to higher strength of motivation. They found, however, no difference between the two groups on McClelland's 'need for achievement' measure, and therefore concluded that the explanation lay not in any motivational difference, but in the predictive limitations of the conventional intelligence test.

Another striking finding in this study was that teachers appeared to approve more strongly of the high IQ group than of the high creativity group. The average rating for 'desirability' as a student' was slightly higher for the former group, even though it was made clear in the rating instructions that 'brightness' was not to be taken specifically into account. Getzels and Jackson comment that the reverse should have been true, since the high IQ groups were only doing scholastically what was expected of them, whereas the high creativity groups (as shown by the achievement results) were doing relatively more than what might have been expected of them. Getzels and Jackson have been criticized (Dunnette 1964, C. P. Butcher, 1970), for making too much of this result. The difference in average rating was apparently not statistically significant, so that the claim should only have been that the high creativity groups were rated no higher than the high IQ groups in spite of their apparent 'overachievement'.

A third respect in which the groups were found to differ was in their attitudes to success in adult life. In the high IQ groups the correspondence between the qualities they valued for themselves and the qualities which they thought would be conducive to success in adult life was quite close. Similarly, there was quite a close correspondence between qualities they said they would like to possess themselves and qualities, they thought teachers tended to approve of. Neither of these correspondences held to nearly the same degree in the 'high creativity' group. In other words, although the 'high creativity' children agreed in general with the 'high IQ' children both about the qualities making for success in adult life and the qualities in pupils that teachers approved of, unlike the 'high IQ' group they were not very interested in these qualities for themselves. One of the qualities the 'creative group' valued considerably more highly than did the 'high IQ' group was the sense of humour.

Getzels and Jackson suggest that the undervaluation of creative children by their teachers was partly accounted for by the less conformist values held by these children. They also describe other differences between the groups besides those reviewed here, and their book includes a great deal of interesting material about these gifted children, such as reproductions of their drawings and extracts from their essays, responses to T.A.T. pictures and autobiographical sketches. Many of these certainly suggest creative talent, and quite a few are skilfully written to amuse.

The research of Getzels and Jackson attracted a great deal of interest and also aroused some controversy. De Mille, R and Merrifield (1962) criticized it quite severely as being ill-designed and inadequately reported. This criticism is largely justified. Often Getzels and Jackson appear only to be reporting what favours their own viewpoint and to be omitting crucial information, such as the characteristics of the children who scored highly in both 'intelligence' and 'creativity'. Their statistical treatment is so sketchy as sometimes to be positively misleading. Furthermore, their contrasting 'high IQ' and 'high creativity' groups were at the extremes in these directions in a sample of children already extreme. Even granted that all Getzels and Jackson's findings were perfectly accurate and fully reported, one would have to be very careful about attempting to generalize from these very exceptional small groups to children outside this range.

A number of writers have suggested that Getzels and Jackson's approach may not be so novel as might be supposed, and that the tests of creativity would, as Burt (1962) put it, 'from very satisfactory additions to any ordinary battery for testing the general factor of intelligence'. The creativity tests in Getzels and Jackson's research did not correlate with each other to a much higher degree than they correlated with IQ, and it is therefore possible to analyse their results further and to show that the creativity tests can be interpreted as partly assessing a factor of general intelligence (Marsh, 1964; Thorndike, 1963).

There have also been several attempts to repeat Getzels and Jackson's work, but with more typical and representative groups of children. These have produced conflicting results. Several of these repetitions have been carried out by Torrance and his associates at the University of Minnesota, and have extended partial support to the Getzels and Jacksons findings that 'creative' children were more successful in school work than could be expected from their IQ. Extensive work into other aspects of creativity has been reported by Torrance, 1959, 1966, 1969; Yamamoto, 1964, 1965. The tests devised by Torrance and his associates have been described and evaluated by Goldman (1964) who has used them for reserch into the creative abilities of English primary school children (Goldman and Clarke, 1967).

Mixed findings have been reported when other proposed tests of creativity have been examined in terms of validity. Mednick (1962) proposed that a test of 'remote associates' would prove effective as an indicator of creative ability. The principle of the test is that the respondent is presented with two or three stimulus words (not obviously connected in sense or association) and is required to find one further word linking them all together. Mednick himself found some positive evidence for the test's validity with two small samples of architecture and psychology students. Findings by Datta (1964; 1964b) and by Andrews (1965), whose criterion was scientific output in terms of patents, published papers and so forth among 1,300 scientists (both academic and industrial), were predominantly negative. Shapiro (1965, 1966), however, has developed two new tests, allied to Mednick's R.A.T., and claims that they have proved useful in identifying creative research scientists.

Ripple and May (1962) rightly point out that the magnitude of the relationship between creativity and intelligence would necessarily be low in groups that do not vary much in IQ. They studied several groups of seventh grade students and gave them various creativity tests, with groups that were homogeneous in intelligence (either all fairly high or all fairly low) IQ and creativity were found to be unrelated. In heterogeneous groups, IQ and creativity were highly related. In the general population, then, IQ is positively related to creativity.

Several of the more recent studies in which attempts have been made to separate creativity from intelligence have been almost completely at variance with the more ambitious claims. Hasan and Butcher (1966) carried out a fairly close repetition of much of the Getzels and Jackson study, but with 175 Scottish children whom, unlike the highly able children tested by Getzels and Jackson, were unselected for ability and approximately representative in this respect of the whole population of secondary school children. Very much more overlap between the measures of intelligence and those of creativity was found than had been reported in the Chicago study. For instance, Getzels and Jackson reported for the boys in their sample a correlation of +·131 between scores on the 'fables' test and IQ. The corresponding correlation found by Hasan and Butcher was +·726. Not all the discrepancies were so large as this, but they were all in the same direction and all substantial. An important additional point is that, although one might suppose the greater overlap between intelligence and creativity in the Scottish study to be a purely statistical effect due to a wider range of ability, this was not the case since there was an equal range of variation in Getzels and Jackson's sample, although the average level was some 25 IQ points higher. Moreover, the large overlap found by Hasan and Butcher was striking. IQ correlated more highly with total 'creativity' score than did 9 out of 10 of the separate 'creativity' tests, even though the latter correlations were part-whole correlations.

When contrasting groups were formed of children scoring high respectively in IQ and on the battery of 10 tests of creativity, those of high IQ scored significantly more highly on two tests of attainment. The Getzels and Jackson finding of teacher preference for intelligent (rather than creative) children was partly confirmed, but it seemed evident in the Scottish survey that it was not the higher 'creativity' as such that resulted in more adverse teacher ratings of desirability as a pupil, but primarily the lower level of intelligence.

Two possible explanations were suggested for these discrepancies. Firstly, there is the plausible 'threshold' suggestion about the relation between general intelligence and creative ability, which suggests that up to a level of about IQ 120 general intelligence is the most important factor, particularly in predicting school achievements, but that at levels about this creative abilities begin to assume more importance (Barron, 1963; McClelland, 1958; Mackinnon, 1962; Meer and Stein, 1955; Yamamoto, 1964; Moore, 1966). This could partly account for the negative findings in the two studies quoted, which both included children in a wide range of ability in non-selective schools. A recent report suggests that new evidence supporting this theory has been amassed by Fuqua (1967). Secondly, Torrance (1965) has found some evidence in his own studies to suggest that differences in school atmosphere and methods of teaching may account for the discrepant results; according to this suggestion the more creative children would be relatively favoured by the more permissive, flexible kind of school environment. It seems unlikely, however, from a consideration of all these researches that a general factor of creativity, if established, will be uncorrelated with general intelligence. It is much more likely to be oblique or correlated, as found by Cropley (1966).

Further light on these conflicting findings has also been thrown by a extensive research reported by Wallach and Kogan (1965). They begin by reviewing earlier reports on the distinction between creativity and intelligence, including the Getzels and Jackson book and papers by Cline, Richards and Needham (1963), Cline, Richards and Abe (1962), Flescher (1963), Torrance (1960), Yamamoto (1964a, b, c), and Guilford (1956, 1959, 1963). Their main conclusion from this survey is that the distinction between creativity and intelligence has not been adequately supported by empirical evidence and that the correlations between measures of 'creativity' are generally lower than those between a typical test of 'creativity' and one of 'intelligence'. They admit to having been disappointed by this general conclusion, but suggest that all the earlier researches reviewed suffered from one particular methodological failing, and that if this is remedied, there may still be hope of maintaining a legitimate distraction between creativity and intelligence. The failing stressed by Wallach and Kogan is the reliance of earlier investigations on group tests administered in a 'psychometric' and usually competitive situation. In contrast, therefore, they took special trouble in their own research to make sure that all the psychological measures were obtained in situations designed to minimize 'test anxiety'. The subjects were 10-11 year-old children, and the experimenters were teachers who had established close rapport with the children and who derived the required data from 'games' and 'lessons' without appearing to upset the normal school programme.

The tests used owed something to Guilford's conceptions. They were measures of associative fluency in response to both verbal and non-verbal stimuli, and were given untimed. There were five of these measures, each being scored separately for number and uniqueness of responses. Wallach and Kogan comment that very few bizarre or inappropriate responses were forthcoming.

Wallach and Kogan have reported a fair degree of success in establishing separate measures of creativity and intelligence in these conditions. What is more, one can assess this progess adequately, as they provide full details, for instance, of the reliabilities and inter-correlations of their measures, they also, where necessry, carry out tests of significance and again provide enough detail for one to see what these are worth. Methodologically their work is far less crude than that of their predecessors. One can therefore put more trust in their claim to have achieved quite a satisfactory practical separation of creativity from intelligence.

Contrasting groups of children were then formed as in the Getzels and Jackson study (but including also groups who were high in both creativity and intelligence or low in both) and were compared on a variety of aspects, including, for instance, attitude to study, degree of social adjustment, level of anxiety and so forth. Wallach and Kogan summarize the main differences between these groups as follows:

High creativity–high intelligence: These children can exercise within themselves both control and freedom, both adult-like and childlike kinds of behaviour.

High creativity–low intelligence: These children are in angry conflict with themselves and with their school environment and are beset with feelings of unworthiness and inadequacy. In a stress-free context, however, they can blossom forth cognitively.

Low creativity–high intelligence: These children can be described as 'addicted' to school achievement. Academic failure would be perceived by them as catastrophic, so that they must continually strive for academic excellence in order to avoid the possibility of pain.

Low creativity–low intelligence: Basically bewildered, these children engage in various defensive maneuvers ranging from useful adaptations such as intensive social activity to regressions such as passivity or psychosomatic symptoms.

Thus, they progressed from the definition and operationalization of two types of cognitive activity to an investigation of their correlates in such areas as observable social and achievement-relevant behaviours, ways of forming concepts, physiognomic sensitivities, and self-described levels of general anxiety, test anxiety, and defensiveness. From the findings obtained, it seems fair to conclude, that the present definition of creativity denotes a mode of cognitive functioning that matters a great deal in the life of the child. Furthermore, consideration of the child's joint status with regard to the conventional concept of general intelligence and creativity as here defined is evidently of critical importance in the search for new knowledge concerning children's thinking.

These summaries, although containing in very condensed form the gist of Wallach and Kogan's findings, hardly do justice to the scope of their work. Many aspects of temperament and personality in this group of children were discussed, and interesting suggestions were made about differing types of conceptualization and classification corresponding to the four groups distinguished. One finding, for instance, was that the high-intelligence, low-creativity group strongly preferred abstract, formal bases of classification. This was not due to inability to use other kinds of category, as Wallach and Kogan showed experimentally, but was interpreted as a kind of defence-mechanism. Similar interesting hypotheses and speculations were advanced about the other three groups. Wallach and Kogan quite correctly point out, however, that even if the findings about creativity in children are valid and come to be generally accepted, there is a particularly large gulf of ignorance about the relation of creativity in children to performance in later life. What is needed, perhaps, is a team like that of Terman and his associates to carry out a large-scale longitudinal study much as he did in the case of intelligence.

Springbelt and others (1957) found significant positive correlation between creativity and intelligence. Ripple and May (1962) correlated the I.Q. scores with creativity scores of seventh grade homogeneous and hetrogeneous groups. They concluded that low correlations between I.Q. and creativity come due to restricted I.Q. ranges in their samples. The correlation between Halstead Tests of higher brain function and the I.Q. scores was significantly low. It was established that Halstead measures something other then conventional I.Q. Jacobson and Asher (1963) reported non-significant correlation between creativity and intelligence. Edward and Taylor (1965) found significantly positive correlation between creativity and intelligence. Clarke and others (1963) studied males and females on I.Q. and creativity tests. A 0.4 correlation between them indicated that creativity and intelligence are independent. Hosan and Butcher (1966) found positive relationship and concluded that in a relatively unselected group measures of convergent and of divergent thinking very largely overlap. Madaus (1967) found negligible relationship between intelligence and creativity over 600 ninth and tenth grade high school students.

Paney and Horrocks (1967) finding creativity in low intelligent 14 boy-scouts of 10-18 years, said main scores were considered lower than normal. Bisenman and Robinson (1967) studied relationship of creativity and intelligence with high school students. They found no relationship between them. Getzels and Jackson (1967) studied the highly intelligent and highly creative adolescents. Iwate (1968) studied relationship of creativity with intelligence and personality variable and they found no relationship between creativity and intelligence and the personality variables.

Ginsburg and Whittemore (1968) found that measures of creativity begin to differ markedly from measures of I.Q. only above a certain level of intelligence. Neuringer (1969) concluded that intelligence has only a minor influence on rating diversity. Day and Langevin (1969) studied curiosity and intelligence, two necessary conditions for high level of creativity. Jacobs (1969) found high intelligence and high creativity intracted.

Some recent studies in this direction are that of Cave, *et al.*, (1970) who studied combined factor analysis of creativity and intelligence and results were compared with various studies. Popescu, Paul and Cornelia (1972) found highly significant correlation between creativity and personality ($P. < .001$); the correlation between creativity and intelligence was not significant ($P > .05$). Johnson, Donald and Max (1974) studied creative aptitudes in a high intelligent population. They found that only 12 of the 66 inter-correlations were high than .30; a major test design objective of achieving sub-test independence was satisfied. Weiman (1975) studied relationship of creativity to intelligence and functional fixedness. Rosseman and Collob (1975) studied comparison of social judgements of creativity and intelligence. They found significant amount of variation unique to creativity judgements which could not be accounted for by intelligence judgements and vice versa. Cooper (1975) studied intelligence, creativity and performance abilities of EMR pupils. They found creativity to be as important as intelligence or more so in determining their rated performance scores. Implications for educational programmes for EMR pupils were also discussed.

Jakhar and Koura (1976-7) found all correlations between creativity and verbal intelligence to be significant while none of the correlations between creativity and non-verbal intelligence reached significance. Hasan and Khan (1976) examined the relationship between creativity, intelligence and temperament. It was found that the inter-correlations among the 3 creativity scores were relatively higher than the correlation of any one of them with intelligence. Singh (1977) studied creativity as related to intelligence, achievement and security–insecurity. They found creativity to be related to achievement and security–insecurity.

Qureshi (1983) also studied the relationship of creativity to intelligence, anxiety and level of aspiration among girls and found it to be significant.

Beside these studies on intelligence and creativity some other studies have been also conducted. Ghassel (1966) found in his study that performance on the test of IQ showed little relation to the performance on the task involving creativity. Thorndike (1963), on the basis of his analysis of the early studies, found that the average correlation among general intelligence test were more related among themselves (0.43) than that found among the tests of divergent thinking (0.27). He further observed that the coefficient between intelligence and divergent thinking tests was 0.24. Further, Thorndike, also reported a low correlation (0.12) between general intelligence and divergent thinking. A comprehensive review of the literature was made by Torrance (1967) who summarized the correlational information in respect of relationship between creativity and intelligence which was observed in a number of studies where his test of creativity was used. He has reported a median value 0.20 for 178 correlation values between intelligence measure and that of composite scores of creativity. The median of 88 correlation coefficient between intelligence and verbal creativity was reported to be 0.21, whereas the median of 114 correlation coefficient between intelligence and figural activity was 0.06. Thus, on the whole creativity and intelligence were found not to be related strongly.

Sharma (1972) in his study on both rural and urban high school sample reported a little rise in creativity with rise in intelligence. Further, he reported a consistent rise in creativity on the lower IQ levels and after 120 IQ creativity reflected inconsistent fluctuations.

The findings of Stone *et al.* (1969) have also reported intelligence and creativity to be positively correlated.

Kovacova *et al.*, (1979) in their study on creative and cognitive processes found no marked relationship between these two variables.

Jersild, *et al.* (1978) have remarked that it would seem that the extent of the relationship between IQs and measured creativity in children depends on the nature of the tests of creativity employed, among other things. The nature of the relationship remains speculative, however. Early speculations that the relationship is slight probably have been exaggerated. Creativity of certain kinds may be highly related to intelligence, whereas creativity in other areas may not depend so much on intelligence. That a rather high level of intelligence is essential for the production of cultural, scientific, technological, or artistic innovation would appear obvious. But a person may have a very high IQ as measured by intelligence tests and still have no flair for the originality and imaginativeness that is characteristic of the creative mind.

Czerwinska, *et al.* (1979) have also reported that intelligence and creativity are two specific mental functions. Riaz and his associates (1979) in their study on eighth grade population, by administering progressive Matrices test of intelligence and the Wallach-Kogan test of creativity, found that creativity and intelligence were independent of each other.

Rawat, M. S. and Agrawal (1977) have also studied the relationship of intelligence and creativity with other variables on an Indian population. They found in their study that high achievers on intelligence were not necessarily high on creativity. However, for girls scores on intelligence affected those on creative thinking.

Singh, R. B. *et al.* (1977) in their study on the relationship of creativity to intelligence and achievement found significant correlation between creativity and intelligence.

However, the study conducted by Schueer *et al.* (1978) compared scores obtained on Torrance test of creative thinking with verbal quotient scores. Their findings confirmed the idea that creativity should be considered as part of intelligence.

This supported the earlier views of Burt (1962) and Vernon, (1964) among others that creativity comes within the vast domain of general intelligence.

Butcher (1968) has suggested that it might be more instructive to treat the distinction between divergent and convergent thinking not as dichotomy but as continuous and to construct test accordingly.

Passi (1962) also noted that intelligence appears to be a significant positive correlate of creativity.

Kumar and Raina (1976) administered the T.T.C.T. (form A), a group test of mental ability, developed by Jalota, a sentence completion measure of achievement mativation to 96 Indian ninth graders. Results showed a significant effect of creativity and intelligence on achievement motivation, but non-significant creativity X intelligence interaction.

Hassan and Khan (1976) conducted a study on 100 male subjects of 12 to 16 years age group. The creativity and intelligence were measured on test of unusual uses and new relationships and Raven's progressive matrices, respectively. The intercorrelations among creativity scores on fluency, flexibility and originality were relatively higher than the correlation of any one of them with intelligence.

Chadda and Sen (1981) conducted a study on 116 students of twelveth grade from Delhi Higher Secondary School. Out of these, 61 were girls and the remaining were boys. Tools employed were T.T.C.T. (Product improvement, unusual uses of cardboard boxes, unusual questions and just suppose activity) Raven's advance progressive matrices and Kulshrestha SES scale. Results showed a significant difference between high creative and low creative boys as well as girls on intelligence. The product moment correlation was also found to be moderate and significantly possible.

Pathak (1962) obtained significant correlation between creativity as measured by the Minnesota non-verbal tests and IQ as obtained on DRAW-a-Man scale.

Paramesh (1971) studied a sample of 100 high school students in the city of Madras on a Wallach and Kogan test of Creativity. The findings indicated that the high, moderate and low creative groups did not significantly differ on age and intelligence.

Dutt *et al.* (1973) conducted a study on 200 male and female students of Delhi to measure creativity in relation to intelligence, extraversion and neuroticism. They observed that these four variables are almost normally distributed. High creative group need not necessarily be highly intelligent.

Sharma (1974) conducted a study on a sample of 414 male urban and rural students. Creativity was measured by the test constructed by the author whereas intelligence was measured by the 'Samuhik Mansik Yogyata Prikshan'. The findings indicated that intelligence is necessary for the development of creative thinking.

Khire (1976) conducted a study on 9–17 years high school students and assessed their intelligence and creativity. Correlation between scores on intelligence and creativity measures were significant but low.

Clark *et al.* (1965) studied males and females on IQ and creativity test and found that these two factors were independent of each other.

Madanawat, A.V. (1986) made a study of creativity in relation to intelligence and manifest anxiety and found that without interaction among themselves, intelligence and anxiety affect fluency, flexibility and originality components of creativity individually and not in interaction with each other.

On the whole, it was found that without interaction among themselves intelligence and anxiety affect creativity individually.

The investigator asserts that the classical relationship between intelligence and creativity has been controverted the main thrust of findings of this study seem to confirm the study on intelligence and creativity.

Along this line of research in India, a comprehensive study on the relationship of intelligence and creativity was conducted by Sajid, S.M. (1984) under the supervision of the present author. He studied the relationship of these two variables on a sample of 400 school students of Mission and Government schools of both the sexes in the State of Bihar. For measuring creativity the tests of verbal and non-verbal creative thinking (Mehdi. B. 1973) were used and for measuring intelligence Mohsin Bihar Test of General Intelligence was used. The researcher analysed the findings by applying correlation and t-ratio. Product moment correlation between scores on intelligence test, interpreted in terms of index of brightness, and scores on various components of verbal and non-verbal creativity were found out. The important findings are as follows.

There is positive and significant relationship between intelligence and flexibility and originality components of verbal test of creativity as well as with the composite scores on it. This suggests that the higher the intelligence the greater the creativity. In the case of non-verbal creativity intelligence was found to be positively and significantly correlated with the elaboration, originality and 'composite scores'. Thus, these correlational findings were indicative of the positive relationship between intelligence and verbal and non-verbal creativity both, except the fluency component on the verbal test of creativity.

Further, the researcher compared the mean scores of high and low creatives (cut-point: median) on intelligence test and the significance value was found out. The findings again indicated the greater intelligence mean scores of high creatives on verbal creativity as compared to their low counterparts (mean value 113.18 and 108.11 respectively-$P<.01$). The mean scores on the basis of non-verbal creativity were 112.41 and 108.64 $P<.05$. This again suggested that high creatives are more intelligent as compared to their low counterparts.

Further, the researcher divided respondents as average and superior with regard to their intelligence and then compared these two groups on verbal and non-verbal test of creative thinking. This was done with a purpose to find out whether intelligence contributes to creativity. The results indicated that subjects obtaining low scores on creativity were low on intelligence. The findings indicated that the superior and average groups in respect of intelligence differed significantly on flexibility and originality as well as on composite scores on verbal creativity. In the case of non-verbal creativity it was found that these two groups did not have a significant difference either in respect of 'elaboration' or 'originality'. However, the subjects of higher intelligence scored higher composite mean scores as compared to that of average intelligence (mean value 103.1 and 97.7 respectively).

Thus, on the whole, the group having superior level of intelligence showed better performance on verbal and non-verbal creativity both, as the composite scores, on these two tests are the addition of the standard scores on the different components of intelligence.

Thus, the comprehensive study of Sajid, S.M. (1984) has supported a number of such studies where it has been shown that intelligence is a necessary component of creativity and it has a positive relationship with creativity. Such related studies are those of Sharma (1974), Stone *et al.*, (1969), Allen, A. *et al.* (1969), Ogilive, E. (1974) Kogan, Pankove (1972); Hudson (1966); Guilford and Christensen (1956); Singh, R.B., Mathur, Sudha, R., Shashi (1977), S. Dias (1976); and Csondorne *et al.*, (1978).

Wallach and Kogan (1965) developed a test a measuring children's creativity and found that they did not correlate with the traditional intelligence test clearly. They remarked that everyone with intelligence quotient over 140 could not be creative. On the other hand, there are persons of average IQ who can contribute to creative work. Anderson (1960) has also remarked that minimal level of ability may be required to carry on a task but beyond that level the performance of an individual is determined by many other factors. Bourne Jr., Bruce. R. (1973) have also remarked in the same direction: 'A minimal amount of intelligence is required for creative output but that is not more than 100 IQ'.

Mackinnon states that creative persons have an unusual capacity to record and retain and have readily available the experiences of their life history. They are observant in a differentiated fashion; they are alert, capable of concentrating attention readily and shifting it appropriately. They have a wide range of information at their command. As in the case of any intelligent person, the items of information which creative person posseses may readily enter into combination since true creativity is defined by the adaptiveness of a response as well as its unusualness. It is apparent that intelligence alone will tend to produce creativity. The more combinations that are found, the more likely it is on purely statistical ground that some of them will be creative (Mackinon, C. F. Freeman, F. S., 1965).

It can be assumed that a fairly high level of intelligence is necessary for creative achievement (Nicholls, 1972). In addition, it has been found that the most creative members of a society are brighter than those who become the leaders of that society (Simonton, 1976).

Thus, intelligence may be considered as necessary condition for creativity, but not the sufficient one. In general, the researches in the field of creativity should not simply aim at exploring a direct relationship of creativity to intellectual components rather personality factors, socio-cultural differences, etc. should also constitute the subject for study. Hence, the studies on intelligence and creativity seem to have paved the way for inclusion of researches on non-cognitive factors as they contribute toward creative performance.

However, the present author feels that still higher and intensive investigations are needed to locate the actual contribution of intelligence to creativity. No doubt, scores on intelligence have been also found in some cases to be positively correlated with those on creative thinking but how can the investigator completely isolate this relationship as other factors like socio-economic status, personality and family environment might contribute something in interaction with one another. These factors should be controlled in order to isolate the effect of intellectual component on creative performance. The author feels on the basis of the review of findings that such perfect controls have not been observed in any of the researches available. Simply by correlating the scores on tests of intelligence with those on creativity how one can generalize the nature of relationship and specially the contribution made by intelligence to creativity. The author does appreciate at the same time the limitations on the part of the researchers while controlling the extraneous variables in psychological researches. This is not true only in the case of the study on intelligence and creativity but with other researches in behavioural sciences. Review of the literature on creativity and intelligence suggests that mostly studies have been made on the basis of the comparison of scores obtained on tests of creativity and intelligence. Very few studies have been conducted on the professional artists and scientists whose creativity cannot be challenged. Naturally, the stereotyped test materials and the performance on the paper pencil test may not present the real creative achievements. Hence, the findings and their interpretations are liable to cast doubts in mind. In the light of the above findings one can safely recognize that intelligence is necessary, if not sufficient and only condition for creative output, and its study has its own place in the field of creativity.

A latest* news title 'Is there genius in mental handicap?' has further complicated the issue and has brought an unusual challenge in the field of creativity and intelligence. The news highlights a recent BBC television programme called 'The Foolish Wise Ones' which supports that there can be genius in mental handicap. The programme examines two cases: Noel Patterson has an extraordinary musical memory. After hearing a tune with complicated harmonies just once, he is able to play it back on the piano with almost total accuracy.

David Kidd, another mentally handicapped, has special talent. Given any date in the past or the future, David can immediately tell on which day of the week it falls.

This is a question which baffles psychologists and neurologists, because Noel and David are not unique. There are other adults and children whose general level of intelligence appears to be so low that they are judged to be mentally subnormal, but who have a single exceptional talent. The above findings have again intensified the need for investigating into the relationship of intelligence to creativity.

***The Hindustan Times*, Aug. 8,1987.

CHAPTER THREE

CREATIVITY IN A FAMILIAL PERSPECTIVE

The review of the literature on creativity clearly suggests the direct bearing of environmental factors on the development and growth of creative potentials. Much has been said empirically as well as theoretically with regard to the role of various environments that are conducive to creative activities. It has already been stated in previous section of this book that 'press' is one of the important strands of creativity. The stimulating and nourishing environment does play a highly significant role in the expression of creative potentials.

Gupta, S. (1986), while speaking at the international conference, said 'creativity is a birthright to every child and it is our belief that every child is creative'. She further stated 'it is our job to help in organizing the right environment for creating something new'. However, it has been pointed out that highly creative children may possibly remain creative even in an uncongenial atmosphere, whereas the potentially creative children need a sympathetic, competitive and stimulating atmosphere to actualize their potential.

Gupta (1976), on the basis of his review, has categorically remarked that understanding of the dynamics of environmental factors constitutes the significant aspect of the study of creativity. The present author feels that creativity is not to be regarded as an inherited trait possessed by only a few children; on the contrary, it seems proper to accept that creative potentials, though different in degree, are present in many children. What they need is the provision for healthy resources and stimulation in the environment in which they are living.

From the very beginning such favourable conditions are to be developed and all attempts should be made to eliminate those situations which may have their adverse effect on the growing child and block the expression of creativity.

The Getzels and Jackson's study, already discussed in connection with intelligence and creativity, suggested certain systematic differences between the high creativity and high intelligence groups in respect of home background and atmosphere. The conclusions suggested that the fathers of the high IQ group tended to be professional people in intellectual occupation, whereas those of the high creativity group were more often in business. They found the mothers of the high IQ group to be less secure and at ease with themselves than those of the high creativity group; in the high IQ group they found both parents tended to be more worried about financial problem, more critical of their children and more worried in general about the dangers of the world. The overall impression of the high IQ family was that it was one in which individual's divergence was limited and risks minimized and that of the high creativity family was that it was one in which individual's divergence was permitted and risks were accepted. Getzels and Jackson also provided two family case histories which presented contrasting atmosphere. Bruner (1961) has stressed the importance of guessing which is a valuable tool in the hands of a thinker. He has suggested that environmental pressure on the child must be such that children be led to master this gift. The environment must permit and entertain the free guessing whether it is silly or brilliant. This indirectly suggests the importance of home and school environment in developing this habit of guessing.

Drevdahl (1964), on the basis of his empirical studies, provided information on the environmental influences playing their role in creative growth. He compared the creative group with that of non-creative in respect of personal, educational and social characteristics as well as experiences. He made comparison between creative and non-creative productive and also between combined controlled groups on motivational analysis test and between creative non-creative, non-productive, non-creative productive and the combined controlled groups on 16PF questionnaire and interview. The findings indicated that parents provided more of educational stimulation to the creative as compared to non-creative productive group. However, the difference was not found to be significant between creative and non-creative, non-productive or combined controlled groups. The creative individuals reflected greater independence in their college life as compared to non-creative non-productive group. However, the significant difference was not found between creative and non-creative productive or combined controlled groups. Further, it was observed that in creative group there was a reflection of stronger attachment and positive feeling toward mother in comparison to father during early life. The creative group was further found to be considerably exposed to reward than punishment as a training device. The intrinsic motivation was found to be of much importance for the creative group than for the non-creative non-productive group.

The dominating nature and personality of the parents have been observed by Cropley (1967) as a source of blocking to the expression of creativity among children.

Before we come to the scientific analysis of the familial factors responsible for creativity it seems proper to mention that in addition to in-home environment the school and the college atmosphere do have their impact on creative behaviour, as the children pass considerable time in their schools and colleges. The type of school in which the individual receives the training has its positive influence on creativity. Snyder, 1967; Mihalevici *et al.*, 1973; Haddon and Litton, 1968; Barker, L. 1970. Moore, 1961; Paradowski, 1967; Karlins and associates, 1967; Worthen, 1968; Williams, 1965; Kogan and Morgan, 1969; Ward *et al.*, 1970; and Johnson, 1973, have observed that the degree of intellectual environment of school has its direct effect on the development and expression of creativity. The child's achievement motivation, interest patterns of other classmates, relationship with the group, immediate and delayed incentives are the significant factors within the subjects and environment which influence the development and growth of creativity.

In schools they are exposed to competitive environment after leaving the protective environment at home. The findings are available which support the positive role of school environment: teachers role and their relationship with pupil, nature of instructional materials and the quality of teaching, unfoldment of patterns of interest as well as the fulfilment of child's needs and motivation. It has been well remarked by a number of investigators that the type of school in which the individual is exposed to training has its strong influence on the unfoldment of his hidden potentials. The school gives a correct direction for the expression of creativity. Heist, 1967; Haddon *et al.*, 1968; Barker, L., 1970; Kaur, 1979 and Snyder, 1967; Moore, 1961; Worthen, 1968; Cartledge, *et al.*, 1969; Ward *et al.*, 1970; Glover, 1973 and many others have categorically remarked that the child's achievement motivation, interrelationship, immediate and delayed incentives provided by the authorities have their bearing on his creative development.

Martynowicz, E. (1965) has reviewed some of the American literature and observed the effective role of personality structure and environmental conditions of the children in shaping their creative endeavour.

Kovacova, Eva (1979) also studied along the same line on the sample of 265 children of 11 years. Out of this sample 60 subjects with high creativity and 60 with low creativity were selected for study. The division of high and low creative group was done on the basis of their scores on Torrance tests of creativity. Further, the two groups were compared on personal data and case study. Factors related to family and school environment contributing towards the development of creativity were isolated. Notable differences were observed between the creative and non-creative groups in respect of environmental characteristics.

On the whole, the environmental conditions fostering creativity have been analysed in terms of time, solitude, encouragement, quality materials, challenging and competitive environment, congenial parent–child relationship, the training procedure, provisions for the acquisition of knowledge and skill, participation in activities which generate interest and reinforce a child for reflecting the hidden creative components. This can be further illustrated as follows : For the development of creative potentials the children must have ample time to play with their ideas and concept in order to give a novel and original form. In the same way the children must be free from the imposition of pressure either by parents or the teachers, as they need ample time and solitude for the development of an enriched and imaginative life. Both the home and school environment must stimulate creative activities by providing correct guidance and encouragement to the children to enable them to use such materials which may enhance the creative endeavour. This type of guidance and encouraging situation are needed from childhood to school years. Children must be in a position to make their creative behaviour enjoyable and socially recognized experience. Further, it has been rightly said that parents must make every effort to make their children independent and self-reliant in order to express their creativity (Hurlock, 1976). As far as the child training procedures are concerned a democratic and permissive child training in home and school are considered to foster creativity. The authoritarian approach may make the child fearful and block his expression. With regard to the acquisition of knowledge, Pulaski (1974) has correctly remarked that children need 'content' in order to fantacise. The greater acquisition of knowledge lays foundations on which the children build their creative potentials. Hence, impoverished environment should not be placed before the children which provides minimum opportunity for the learning of skills.

Hurlock (1978) has observed non-intellectual factors like inappropriate educational and vocational goals, fear of criticism, poor economic status and other unresolved problems in diverting even the intellectually gifted creative children from full expression of their talent.

In the light of aforesaid discussion on the role of environment in shaping the creative growth one can easily appreciate the vital role of family in this direction. Family has been always considered to be the first and the foremost institution of learning and training. Home is the starting point in the life of a man and factors associated with this environment have been found to affect the development of creativity. The roles played by 'broken home' and a healthy home are well recognized by psychologists. Hurlock (1956) has correctly remarked that the kind of home will have a marked influence on the child's whole outlook towards life. McGuire (1952) has also argued in favour of distinct influence of family life upon the things, persons and ideas one perceives, upon his attachment and also on his mode of evaluation of experiences. Variation in family background leads to the variation in learning situation.

Thus, on the whole the arguments are in favour of the greater influence of the family when one considers non-scholastic forces behind achievement. Hence, favourable conditions conducive to the growth of creativity must be established from the early span of life within the family itself. Keeping these facts in mind various researchers have explored the familial background factors behind creativity. Sajid, S.M. (1984); Sharan, P. (1986) on the basis of the review of literature as well as their own research findings have well emphasized the role played bv familial factors in fostering the growth of creative potentials. They have extensively studied a number of familial variables associated with creativity. The familial factors commonly include parental education and their involvement in creative and stimulating activities; their mode of exercising discipline and reward and punishment, recognition of child's assets and limitations and his search for independence, the healthy and congenial relationship between parents and children, sibling relations, impossessive and democrotic atmosphere, family outlook, socio-economic status, presence/absence of parents and many other such factors which contribute toward children creative growth. The empirical studies of Roe, 1972; Weisberg and Springer, 1961; Cross, 1966; Cropley 1967; Shafer and Anastacy, 1968 have indicated that family background, position of the family and mutual respect for the family members at home, and in community, feeling of being worthy, social and intellectual bases in the family and also the professional background of the parents contribute towards the child's creativity.

In addition to such factors various fascets of in-home behavioral environment like child rearing practices, socio-economic condition, size of the family, joint/nuclear family, liberal/conservative outlook etc. may determine the growth of creative components within the individuals.

Harvey *et al.* (1961) have well reviewed the effect of home environment on creativity by considering the organizational patterns and degree of conceptualization within individual as the two basic qualities of the environment. Low conceptualization of a person is reflected in his stereotyped thinking whereas high conceptualization is manifested in terms of exploration of new situation to be creative.

Sibling relations, feeling of being isolated during childhood and unbroken homes have been also found to influence creative growth in the studies of McClelland (1956), and Oden (1968). Studies are also available indicating that parent-child relationship, over-protectiveness exercised by the parents, recognition for autonomy and non-conformity and also for child's individuality and ability, parental tolerance and self-control also have their positive effects on the development of creativity in children (Crutchfield, 1962; Mackinnon, 1962; Drevdehl 1964; Wyner, 1967; Spotts and Macler 1967; Aldous, 1973-1975).

Eisenman and Foxman (1970) in their studies on college students observed that those who spent maximum time with both the parents were found to be more creative as compared to those who had an opportunity to live with either of the parents for longer duration. The parental love and affection determined the growth of individual intellectually. Singh, R. (1980) in his study on students found that education, occupation and income of the father were quite significant in determining the growth of creativity. The creative group was found to be superior to the non-creative group, categorized on the basis of the scores on Torrance test of creativity, in respect of these three variables. Results also suggested that the creative group belonged to upper socio-economic class.

Jarial (1981) compared the creativity scores of the respondents coming from small, average and larger families. Those who belonged to the small families were found to be significantly superior in comparison to the members of average and large families on scores on fluency and flexibility components of creativity.

Socio-economic status of family has been also extensively studied and reviewed by a number of researchers. The term socio-economic status refers to an individual's position in a society which is determined by wealth, occupation and social class (English and English, 1958). In other words socio-economic status is conceived as a combination of multiple factors that serve as an index of the position of the individual's family in the society. These factors may be education, occupation, and income. Elliott and Merrill (1947) treat 'status' as the position occupied by the individual in the group by virtue of his sex, age, family, class, occupation, marriage and achievement. Reviewing literature on socio-economic status, Sharan, P. (1986) has clearly remarked that socio-economic status is a mental construct, a degree of esteem or disesteem which people in a society display towards individual person. High socio-economic status, therefore, points toward a person's high income, high occupation and adequate living conditions, whereas, the low socio-economic status refers to poor income, low occupation and inadequate living condition. High socio-economic status is considered to make provision for healthy and enriched stimulating environment in which personality can have its all-round development. Whereas children of low income group may develop feeling of insecurity and inferiority and unhealthy attitude toward people and objects. Hurlock (1956)has also observed a marked difference in behaviour pattern in families of different socio-economic groups. However, the definite role of this variable in fostering the growth of creativity is still controversial, though studies supporting the advantage of high socio-economic status are greater in number. Bless, W. *et al.* (1981) studied creativity in this direction and found that socio-economic status was positively related to creativity. Ahmad 1980; Vijay Lakshmi, 1980; Sajid, S.M. 1984; Sharan, P. 1985 have also observed in their study that respondents belonging to a family enjoying high socio-economic status, excelled on measures of creativity.

Khatana, 1971; Ward and Cox, 1974; Singh, 1978; Srivastava, 1978; Sharma, 1980; Gupta, 1976 and Earl, 1973 have also observed socio-economic status of the parents to have quite significant positive effect on creativity of the respondents.

Forman, Susan, G. (1979) examined the effect of socio-economic status on creative performance on a sample of elementary school children. Wallach-Kogan measure of creativity, primary mental ability test and sub-tests from the IOVTA test of basic skills were administered to a sample of 129 second grade students; results indicated that upper class subjects scored better than their lower class counterparts on the test of creativity, but when IQ or achievement was co-variated, this difference was not found to be significant.

Ward, William, *et al.* (1974) also conducted two empirical studies in order to examine whether creative performance could be attributed to the sex or the socio-economic status of the respondents. The findings indicated no sex difference in respect of creativity, but SES was found to be significantly associated with creative performance for those tasks to which at least a moderate amount of effort had been devoted.

Northway and Rookes, 1956; Zeleney, 1956; and Janssen, 1968 have also laid emphasis on the significant role of SES on the development of hidden creativity of children.

Bless, W. *et al.* (1981) have also studied the relationship between creativity and social-status on a sample of 160 Czechoslovakian undergraduate students. Results showed that clear-cut relation was not found between creativity and status but positive relations were found to dominate.

Bhardwaj, R.L. and Gupta, R.P. (1980) examined the respondents' interest in scientific pursuits, as it relates to fluency, intelligence and socio-economic status. Findings indicated that only 'fluency' as a whole and as associational tended to promote or denote interest in scientific pursuits under different levels of intelligence and SES. Intelligence plays an important role when socio-economic status is observed to be quite different.

Singh, R.J. (1980) while studying 178 students–teachers made comparisons between creative and non-creative group with regard to the family background. The findings revealed that the so-called creative group tended to be superior to the non-creative group in terms of education, occupations and income of the father. Results, thus, indicated that persons higher on creativity usually came from upper socio-economic status.

Singh (1978) in a cross-cultural study of creative abilities found that socially disadvantaged children, regardless of culture, did not score low on verbal test of creativity and with the increasing socio-economic status, abilities such as flexibility and originality excelled.

The studies conducted by Sharan, P. 1986 and Sajid, S.M. 1984 are more illustrative. The studies were conducted under the supervision of the present author. Sharan, P. (1986 in her study on 400 college students has reported a positive and significant correlation of SES with verbal and non-verbal creativity ($r = .630$ and $\cdot 417$ respectively $P < \cdot 01$). The SEs was measured by Sharma socio-economic status scale and creativity by Mehdi test of verbal and non verbal-creativity. Sajid. S.M. (1984) has reported a positive and significant relation of SES with flexibility, originality components of creativity and also with composite scores on creativity, ($r = \cdot 11, \cdot 31$ and $\cdot 18$ respectively). However, the relationship was not significant in the case of fluency. As far as nonverbal creativity is concerned, the SES was positively and significantly correlated with elaboration and also with composite scores ($r = 0\cdot 17$ and $0\cdot 13$). The 'originality' component did not show significant relationship with SES. Further, the researcher compared the high and low creative groups, categorized on the basis of the median of composite scores on creativity measure, on their mean scores obtained on socio-economic status scale. The findings showed that the high creatives scored greater mean scores on Socio-Economic status as compared to their low counterparts. The differences between the means of the two groups were also significant. Thus, the two research findings reported above also support the notion that high socio-economic status contribute positively to the growth of creative potentials. The probable reason supporting this finding is that such families of high SES are in a position to manage far greater resources, challenging and facilitating environment which proves to be quite conducive to the children for exploring and reflecting their creative assets lying within. The better socio-economic condition provides a nourishing environment in home and also facilitates a better schooling and acquisition of requisite materials for the expression of creative potentials.

On the other hand, the findings of Raina (1968) and Awasthi

(1979) suggest that creative individuals come from families having average socio-economic status. Bless, W. *et al.* (1981) have reported that in their studies on creativity and socio-economic status the relationship was not found to be clear-cut, though positive trend predominated. Forman, Susan, G. (1979), while investigating into the effect of socio-economic status on creativity in elementary school children, by administering the Wallach–Kogan test of creativity and primary mental ability test, reported on the basis of multi-variate ANOVA that subjects belonging to upper class scored better on measures of creativity than those who belonged to lower class. However, when IQ or achievement level was co-varied the difference between the subjects belonging to upper and lower class was not significant.

In addition to the study of socio-economic status as a variable in creativity Sajid, S.M. (1984) and Sharan, P. (1986) have exclusively studied a number of other familial background factors in order to examine their role in creative development. The present author supervised these two researchers.

These two investigators gathered information in respect of family structure (joint/nuclear family) parental participation in creative activities and hobbies, conservative/liberal outlook of the family and other such factors. These constituents of family environment were then associated with verbal and non-verbal creativity in order to examine, if there exist any relationship between these two sets of variables.

The study was conducted on samples of 400 school students by Sajid, S.M. (1984) and Sharan, P. (1986) separately.

The relationship between the familial factors and verbal and non-verbal creativity was examined by applying chi-square technique. This technique was used in order to find out whether high and low creative groups could exhibit some association with the familial background factors. The details are presented as follows:

The association between joint/nuclear family structure and creativity was studied with the assumption that joint family provides an opportunity for competitive behaviour, exchange of thought, greater stimulation, excitement, diversified activities and decision-making behaviour which may extend facilitation for exhibiting creative potentialities. Sajid, S.M. has reported chi-square value ·162 and 1·023 for verbal and non-verbal creativity respectively. These values were not statistically significant. Thus, the researcher gathered that the joint/nuclear family structurecould not be taken as differentiating factors with regard to creative development. Thus, the hypothesis was not tenable.However, Sharan, P. while repeating the same study on the school sample observed chi-square value (4·09, 15·92) to be significant at ·05 and ·01 level of confidence, which indicated that verbal and non-verbal creativity both are associated with the joint/nuclear family structure. The analysis of cell frequencies also indicated, on the whole, that the number of high creatives was greater in the cells meant for joint family. Thus, this findings supported the assumption that joint family facilitates the creative development more as compared to nuclear family by way of providing a better competitive environment. The joint family system extends an opportunity to the individual for satisfying his needs to excell, compete and learn through joint living and interactions of thoughts of which he is devoid of, to a greater extent, in a nuclear family set-up. The joint family living helps an individual in raising his level of tolerance and aspiration, amidst frustration and denials which in turn help in becoming a matured and balanced personality which facilitates creative involvement. Further, it is held that joint family provides lesser opportunity for the satisfaction of individual's varied wants hence he satisfies his internal wants through sublimating his desires and becoming indulged in creative activities. However, the author who himself supervised these two researchers does not feel comfortable to generalize either of the findings and puts this problem open to further researches because of controversial results.

Another familial variable taken by these two researchers was liberal/conservative or non-traditional/traditional family-outlook as facilitating or inhibiting factor in creative growth. This problem was taken on the assumption that in conservative families the scope for deviation and innovation of ideas and thoughts is less. The liberal outlook invites innovation and novelty and reinforces this innovation and divergence which culminate in creative thinking. In traditional families, on the other hand, the old values are retained and there is lesser exposition to novel and deviating thoughts and actions which may block the development of creative growth. However, Sajid, S.M. (1984) has cautioned against this generalization on the rationale that families having traditional mode of living have been found to produce creatives in the field of dance, music, sculpture, painting and many other such artistic activities. The findings of Sajid, S.M. (1984) on this issue have shown that there was non-significant association between high and low verbal creativity and traditional/non-traditional family outlook. The obtained chi-square value (0·097) was not significant even at .05 level. The examination of the cell frequencies also indicated a lesser difference in respect of frequency of traditional and non-traditional family set-up of high and low creative groups. However, on non-verbal creativity the high and low scorers differed with regard to the traditional and non-traditional mode of living. The chi-square (4.04) was also significant, which indicated a strength of association between high and low creativity and the traditional/non-traditional family set-up. The study of cell frequencies also manifests that the number of high scorers was greater in cell meant for non-traditional family and lesser in the cell meant for traditional one in comparison to their low counterparts. Sajid, S.M. has well argued in support of this finding. The possible explanation for the non-verbal creativity to be associated with non-traditional family may be that, for the growth of creative activities like dance, drama, painting, sculpture, etc. the traditional/non-traditional family has its impact whereas for verbal creativity to grow what one requires are abstraction of ideas, fluency, flexibility and originality with verbal materials which might be generated by number of variables and not simply by traditional/non-traditional mode of family living.

However, the findings of Sharan, P. (1986) in respect of the same variable (liberal/conservative family) have yielded a significant chi-square value indicating strength of association between this familial variable and that of creativity in the case of both verbal and non-verbal. The study of various cell frequencies also indicated that greater number of high scorers on creativity belonged to liberal family whereas the low scorers had greater frequency in cell meant for conservative family.

Thus, the superiority of liberal family outlook has been confirmed by both the researchers in the case of higher non-verbal creativity, though, controversy lies in the area of verbal creativity. Hence, again the author suggests for taking up further researches on this specific problem.

Further, the researchers also attempted at finding out if there exist any relationship between an individual's creative endeavour and the parental involvement in creative activities. This step was taken under the assumption that creative potentials within the children can get their expression smoothly in an environment which is charged with creative interest and involvement. The parental involvement or that of other family members in creative activities can facilitate the creative thinking of the children and encourage them to take up creative work. Sajid, S.M. (1984) and Sharan, P. (1986) both reported a significant association of the creative/non-creative parental interest and the high and low non-verbal creativity of children. The obtained chi-square values 7.425 and 8.92 respectively were significant at ·01 level. However, in the case of verbal creativity Sajid, S.M. has reported a non-significant relationship (chi-square = 1.023) whereas Sharan, P. obtained a significant relationship (chi-square = 14·13).

However, Sajid, S.M. too observed that superficially the high scorers on verbal creativity represented greater frequency in the cell, indicated for creative involvement of the parents as compared to their non-creative involvement. The investigator (Sajid, S.M.) supported the present findings in respect of verbal creativity by giving a simple explanation in terms of abstraction. and non-abstraction. On the test of verbal creativity the respondents are required to think various consequences of the specific situation which demands his ability to retrieve items of information out of the storage of personal information which finally measures his ability to shift his frame of reference. The verbal test of creativity employed in this research also provides an opportunity to the individual to play of his imagination freely and adding many new things. It is also a measure of individual's sensitivity towards problems associated with fluency and flexibility of thinking, originality of responses, redefinition of familiar objects and elaboration of ideas. However, one should remember that items on the non-verbal test of creativity do measure such components of creativity but emphasize the exercise with figural content in a creative way, and thus, provide an opportunity to think with some figural task and come out with some novel and unique product. What the researcher wants to emphasize is that the parental involvement in creative art may facilitate children's non-verbal creativity easily but not the verbal one which needs abstraction of ideas associated with verbal materials and task. The non-verbal creative activities are easier to be imitated. Further, explanation for the greater influence of parental creative activities on non-verbal creativity of their children has been that the sample of study mostly included such parents who displayed the creative activities of non-verbal nature which had, in turn, its effect on the non-verbal creativity of children. Hence, the findings cast doubt to an extent and suggest further studies on samples which represent parental interest in verbal creativity also so that it could be examined whether such environment would also influence the verbal creativity of children.

However, Sharan, P. (1986) has reported significant association (chi-square = 14.13 $P < \cdot 01$) between parental involvement in creative activities and higher verbal creativity of their children. Thus, on the whole the family environment has been found to affect creativity of children.

However, one should keep in mind that highly creative children excell on creativity even though the circumstances in the family are not very conducive. Drevdahl (1964) and Barron, 1962; have also pointed towards this fact when they remarked that there are instances where exceptionally creative individuals have excelled in creative activity amidst adverse circumstances, as they have intrinsic motivation to excell and need for actualization and high ego strength.

While investigation into the familial undercurrents of creativity Sajid, S.M. and Sharan, P. also included the study of the relationship between the respondents' preference for creative and non-creative hobbies and their performance on test of verbal and non-verbal creativity. The underlying assumption was that the indulgence in creative hobbies may generate more and more creative interest within the individual. The very indulgence in creative hobbies and activities points toward the fact that a person is moving in a creative direction. The findings of Sajid, S.M. and Sharan, P. indicated a significant chi-square value (31·640 and 29·51 respectively) indicating association between the respondents' nature of hobbies and their performance on non-verbal test of divergent thinking, However, Sajid, S.M. has reported a non-significant association between the nature of hobbies and the verbal creativity (chi-square = 0·866). On the other hand Sharan, P. has reported a significant and strong association between these two variables (chi-square = 85.41). Sajid, S.M. has extended his argument for explaining the non-significant association in the area of verbal creativity. He has stated that the development of verbal creative activities may not be simply associated with the respondent's preoccuption with creative hobbies like music, painting, drama, potry, etc. as it also needs manipulation of abstract ideas and verbal materials. The fluency, flexibility and originality aspects of creativity seem to be difficult to be generated simply by being involved in some creative hobbies. Such hobbies may affect the acquisition and expression of non-verbal creative behaviour more easily as it requires mainly manipulation of figures and drawings given in the test. Thus, even simple stimulation for non-verbal creative work can generate interest in it. Thus, again the controversy with regard to the impact of creative hobbies on verbal creativity of the subjects is to be solved by conducting further researches, specially on those samples who are professionally engaged in creative work.

Sharan, P., further examined factors like presence/absence of parents as well as siblings; reward/punishments, care/negligence, relative preference for father and mother; own/step mother peaceful/disturbed home environment and feeling of being respected and valued in comparison to other siblings. The findings along with their interpretations are worth mentioning in order to appreciate how even a minor thing in the family can facilitate/hinder the growth of creative potentials.

Presence/absence of father and creativity:

The study was conducted to test the underlying assumption whether presence/absence of father contributes to the development of creativity of children. The parental figure is a source for the provision for educational facilities, emotional bonding and proper guidance. He serves as a model for identification during socialization of the child. Father's love and affection affect children's need for love and adjustment positivity. Father serves as reinforcer for the intellectual, social and imaginative attainments of the child. The findings however, indicated a non-significant relationship between presence/absence of father and the high and low scores on verbal creativity, whereas this association was significant in the case of non-verbal creativity. The examination of the cell frequency also indicated association between low creativity and absence of father figure. The findings of Eiseman and Foxman 1970 have also indicated that the children who had an opportunity to pass most of their time with both the parents were more creative.

Further, in her study on own/step mother as a familial variable in creativity, Sharan, P. (1986) observed a significant association between these two variables on the test of non-verbal creativity. However, a significant association could not be observed in the area of verbal creativity, as the chi-square value (·015) was not significant even at ·01 level of confidence. The overall examination of the cell frequencies also indicated less differences between the cell frequencies of own/step mother of high and low creative groups. The maternal figure has always been considered to be a source of satisfaction of emotional needs and imaginative growth, which serve as reinforcer for the expression of creative potentials within the children. Such reinforcements lack either due to death of mother or separation from father. This is further affected by the arrival of step-mother in home. That is why, the investigator was interested in analysing creativity with regard to presence/absence of own mother and presence of step mother. This might have facilitating or inhibiting effect on the development of children's constructive components.

The findings indicated that the high and low creative groups exhibited association with this variable significantly only on non-verbal creativity. The lack of this significant association on verbal creativity points towards the fact that it is not only the presence of step mother which counts but the degree of love and affection shown by her to children counts more. Hence, the presence of step mother may not be considered as the only force behind lack of creative behaviour in children. However, with the researcher's further attempt on healthy/unhealthy relationship with the step mother and development of creative growth could not yield a significant relationship as the chi-square values were not significant in the case of verbal and non-verbal creativity both. So the findings extend partial support to the assumption that presence of own/step mother could act as a powerful determinant of creativity.

Another familial variable which had been studied was the care and supervision received by children in home. The feeling of being neglected or less cared may have its diverse and distructive effect on children. The children do identify themselves with their parents and expect all possible protection and care from them. The parents play important role in generating confidence and self respect in their children. Their proper attitude can motivate and encourage the child. On the other hand, if the child feels neglected or least cared, he may develop hostility and aggression and also sometimes inferiority feeling which might block his movement in a creative and constructive direction. Such feelings may result in the development of psycho-pathological behaviour pattern and maladjustment which may not be considered healthy for fostering the growth of creative potentials. However, at this point of discussion, it may be pointed out that such pathological feelings, resulting from the sense of being isolated and neglected, may have their expression in some creative work, though of different quality. The parental care and love for children help their offsprings in accepting their values and interests enthusiastically with open-mindedness (Getzels and Jackson, 1961).

Weisberg and Springer (1961) also observed the favourable and encouraging aspect of warm and intense relationship among parents and children in the development of creative potentials. Drevdahl (1964) has also reported that the creative group in his study displayed a stronger attachment to and positive feelings towards the mother as compared to non-creative group of subjects. The empirical findings of Sharan, P. (1986) further extended support to this fact as the high and low scorers on creativity displayed a significant association with the parental care and attachment in the area of verbal and non-verbal creativity both as the chi-square values were significant at ·01 level of confidence.

One important variable in the area of familial undercurrents is the effect of the exercise of reward and punishment in the family on verbal and non-verbal creativity of children. It is generally held that reward is a powerful incentive which generates an intense desire for the acquisition and exploration of knowledge and skill in children. The rewarded group has been observed to be inspired for greater achievement whereas the non-rewarded feels degenerated and discouraged. The punishment plays more damaging role in achieving creative attainment. Drevdahl (1964) has emphasized the positive role of reward in generating creative endeavour. The studies of Feld (1967) have also stressed the encouraging role of reward in creative work. The studies conducted by Sharan, P. (1986) have also shown that the high and low creative groups, categorized on the basis of their scores on test of creativity, showed a significant association with the respondent's feeling of being rewarded/unrewarded and also that of punished/unpunished, as the chi-square values were observed to be significant at ·01 level of confidence in all the cases. The high creative groups had greater frequency in the cell containing frequencies on being rewarded and not punished as compared to their low counterparts. Thus, on the whole, reward most favourably affects the growth of creativity in children whereas punishment has more deterring effect. Punishment has been found to be more damaging in comparison to being unrewarded.

Presence of siblings in the family has been also taken as a familial variable in the area of creativity. A child is inspired and stimulated if he is put in the company of other siblings who make the family environment more competitive and argumentative. The presence of siblings provides an opportunity for greater interaction and exchange of opinion. The single child in the family generally finds himself to be isolated and gets minimum opportunity within the family for imitating the behaviour of others. Further, there is a lack of emotional support and participation in the absence of brothers and sisters. For the purpose of exploration and interchangability of opinion and thought one needs company. The sibling rivalry has been observed by Hurlock (1978) to be a potent factor behind curricular and co-curricular achievement of the child. Such achievements are modified and improved by the sense of competition in the child. The siblings facilitate the smooth and adequate socialization and purposeful achievements which are supposed to contribute positively to creative activities of children. The presence of siblings provides an opportunity for evaluating one's own behaviour. All such opportunities facilitate the acquisition of skills and arousal of motive for creative work. The findings of Sharan, P. (1986) have also empirically supported the facilitating effect of presence of siblings on the development of hidden creative components (verbal and non-verbal creativity both). The chi-square values (21·92and 5·15) have been reported to be significant at ·01 level in verbal and non-verbal creativity both, which indicate a strong association between presence/absence of siblings and creativity of a child. The researcher has also reported that the number of subjects of high creative group was greater in the cell meant for presence of siblings where as the frequency that of low scorers was greater in the cell meant for absence of siblings. Thus, the creative endeavour has its faster growth in the company of other siblings.

One more related familial variable affecting creativity has been the 'emotional bonding' between the parents and their offsprings. It is commonly held that the greater the emotional attachment between the parents and the offsprings, the greater the sense of belongingness, identification, security and protection as well as a desire for moving ahead within the children. Getzels and Jackson, 1961; Wersberg and Springer, 1961; Mackinnon, 1962 and Drevdahl, 1964 hold the opinion, on the basis of their studies, that parental care, emotional attachment and affectionate behaviour motivate children for getting involved in creative pursuits. Sharan, P. (1986) also studied this factor by comparing the number of high and low scorers on test of creativity in three cell frequencies representing high, low and moderate emotional attachment of the respondents to their parents. The chi-square values were found to be significant at ·01 level on verbal and non-verbal creativity both. The statistical results indicated that the number of high creatives was maximum in the cell of high 'emotional bonding'; the next higher frequencies were in the cell of high emotional bonding; the next higher frequencies were in the cell meant for moderate bonding; whereas the lowest was in that of low emotional bonding. The findings presented just opposite picture when the cell frequencies were compared taking low creative groups into consideration. Thus, the findings supported the facilitating effect of stronger emotional attachment on the creative performance of the respondents. The greater emotional attachment provides a greater opportunity for the display of creative potentials in a congenial and affectionate atmosphere.

Another familial variable included in the study of creativity is peaceful/disturbed family environment and its effect on the development of creativity. It is generally presumed that healthy environment facilitates the smooth functioning of an individual in a desired direction. The family members live in peace having respect for mutual understanding and find it easier to actualize their potentials by involving themselves in constructive imaginative works. On the other hand, a disturbed family environment has its adverse effect on the growth of personality. The peaceful environment might affect the expression of creative thinking and intellectual development beside social and emotional growth, whereas the disturbed home environment may block the proper concentration on the problems and hinder the expression of creative potentials. It has been rightly remarked that a healthy environment produces a constructive mind whereas the tension prevailing among the family members, unwanted criticism, provocating remarks, jealousy and other such factors of disintegration are considered to be disrupting agents for creative reflections. This connotation points towards the healthy effect of a nourishing environment on the development of creative talents. This has been supported by the findings of Sharan, P. (1986) who examined the strength of association between high and low creativity and the healthy/unhealthy familial environment, resulting from peace and disturbances respectively in the family. She has reported significant association between these two sets of variables (chi-square values 83·72 and 10·62 respectively for verbal and non-verbal creativity).

Another familial variable which has been reported in the literature on creativity is the child's feeling of commanding respect and recognition in comparison to other siblings in the family. This is a common observation that within the same family structure all children do not have the feeling of equal treatment. Sometimes the parents show a differential treatment either consciously or unconsciously. If the child develops a feeling of being less cared in comparison to other siblings it may affect his healthy and constructive socialization which is the foundation-stone of any intellectual and creative pursuit. The child may have feeling of inferiority resulting in defiance and aggression which prove to be harmful to the development of personality, as a whole. He may not feel encouraged and inspired by the parents or other parental figures. This affects adversely the establishment of emotional bonding and constructive approach toward any problem. However, the present author argues that it is wrong to generalize that children having feeling of being isolated, unrecognized and ill-cared, cannot reflect their creative genius. They may exhibit their talents but in a different direction, reflecting the type of care which they have received and the feelings which they have developed. There are paintings and poems which represent excessive aggression, sadism, and masochism as well as harsh criticism. Such works are also considered to be creative if they are novel and unique. However, what is to be more emphasized is that a healthy and peaceful family environment may be more conducive and encouraging for the exploration and creation of something in a constructive fashion. Many individuals may not express their creative potentialities if they are exposed to unhealthy and disturbed family environment.

This fact has been well substantiated by Sharan, P. (1986) in her study on 400 college students. She compared the high and low scorers on creativity in the light of the magnitude of their feeling of being respected and valued in comparison to other siblings. The responses were categorized in 3 categories: feeling of receiving more, less and equal treatment. The chi-square values (46·04 and 52·88) for verbal and non-verbal creativity respectively) were reported to be significant at ·01 level which indicated a strong association between high and low creativity and the magnitude of the feeling of being respected in the family. Thus, the child's feeling of how much he is respected by his parents and other family members and the way in which his-feelings are responded to has its impact on his creative performance. The investigator has also analysed the different cell frequencies and found that a higher percentage of the high creative group had a feeling that they were more respected as compared to other siblings. The next higher percentage was in the cell ment for 'equal treatment', and the least was in the cell displaying the frequency of respondent's feeling of least cared and respected by the parents. This empirically shows that feeling of being respected and cared for becomes reinforcer in itself for the expression of creativity. This finding has its support from Mackinnon, 1962; Crutchfield, 1962; Drevdahl, 1964; Feld, 1967; Bishop and Chase, 1971, who have advocated, on the basis of their findings, that parental attitude toward their children, their love, affection and care for them proved to be a good impetus for taking up intellectual and creative pursuits.

Thus, while going through the literature in the area of creativity the author came across a number of theoretical and empirical approaches toward the role of familial background factors in facilitating or hindering the growth of creative performance. The author has marked that studies conducted by Sajid, S.M., 1984 and Sharan, P., 1986 have covered such minute details in respect of familial influence which have not probably been included by any other single researcher. The studies, on the whole, have well substantiated various assumptions regarding the role of familial factors as reinforcers to creative growth and development. And thus, it can be well stated that in spite of presence of creative potentials lying within the individual the family contributes something more significant for their expression and channelization. That is why, the study of creativity in a familial perspective has been given due importance.

CHAPTER FOUR

CROSS-CULTURAL STUDIES ON CREATIVITY

The cultural or economic development in itself does not play significant role in the development of creative potentials, what is more important is independence of thought and action enjoyed by the individuals in a culture.

Stein (1960) has well remarked that the extent to which different creative works are generated and produced depend on the extent to which cultural influences permit the development of freedom between the individual and environment as well as within one's own self. The creative endeavour depends on how much diversity and ambiguity are encouraged and tolerated by the specific culture. Cultures which appreciate and recognize the diversities in individual's thoughts and actions naturally reinforce for introducing something unique and novel. In this context one is reminded of the saying that it is the culture which transmits uniformity in ideology and overt actions. That is why, if some challenges are made by way of producing something unusual or deviating, it is generally not appreciated by the culture. However, this is also a fact that the social changes which take place are the results of deviation from the prescribed mode of cultural values. Thus, creative works should be recognized by specific culture in order to further reinforce such endeavours.

Further, the cultural way of living may reinforce the reflection of creative potentials. An individual being a member of the cultural group can even develop his creativity by way of his participation in the cultural activities of his group. If the culture has rich heritage and creative display it is expected to generate creative interests.

With this note one comes across two main aspects of the study of creativity in a cultural perspective. Firstly, the differences, if any, found between the subjects of two diffent cultures may be interpreted in terms of the prevailing creative atmosphere within a culture and to what extent a specific culture is ready to encourage the novelty and uniqueness in action and thoughts of its members.

The cultural variations may be in terms of geographical, psychological and social environment. The variation may be attributed to child-rearing practices, rituals, beliefs, norms and overt action patterns. In short, creativity can also be affected by cultural variations in terms of its various facets. Cultural environment, thus, can be taken as a factor in creative output.

The term culture refers to various meanings. It may cover people of different countries, religions, geographical background, socio-economic status and observing different customs, rituals, standards and values. One cultural group has its distinct identity because of its following of specific ideology. It has been rightly said that while studying culture of a group, one must appreciate the implicit and explicit character of it. Implicit culture refers to the ideology and belief system which serve as undercurrents of behaviour and resulting in uniformity of thought, on the other hand, the explicit culture is reflected in terms of standard behaviour pattern which is guided by established norms and code of conduct. The members of one culture try to conform to their cultural demands and exhibit behaviour in that direction. Hence, the underlying demands of one cultural group guide an individual's behaviour and action tendencies. Every culture provides different environment and patterns of living and growth under which an individual has to promote his living standard. Piddington (1950) has referred to some main contents of a culture which cover geographical environment, political organization, economic system, education, religion, art, recreation, ceremonial functions, material acquisition, norms and social organization.

White (1959) referred to ideological, sociological, sentimental, attitudinal and technological components of culture.

On the whole, one can recognize the physical and psychological components of a culture.

Sharma, K.N. (1979) while reviewing literature on culture, has referred to the views of a number of researchers, in support of his argument in favour of cultural influence on creativity. He has referred to various components of culture and also considered various sub-grouping within the main culture. He considered culture to be a multi-model complex. It may include geographical variablity in respect of province, hilly lands, deserts, planes, sea coast, etc; religious groupings in terms of underlying religious beliefs and rituals, linguistic groupings and professional groupings etc. Thus it is to be noted that a broad culture of any country may consist of many independent cultural groups exhibiting distinct patterns of thoughts and behaviour.

The cultural atmosphere provides a famework within which cognitive abilities can develop. In a provocative article Bruner (1964) discussed an important aspect of outside influence, the culture, as an important interacting factor in cognitive development. He has stated that the development of human intellectual functioning, from infancy to such perfection as it may reach, is shaped by a series of technological advances. Growth depends upon the mastery of techniques and skills involved in it. These techniques are not within the main inventions of the individuals who are growing up they are rather skills transmitted with varying effectiveness and success by the culture.

This has been clearly remarked that the characteristics of infancy are universal. Culture begins to extend its effect during the early training process and overlays or modifies a more basic sub-stratum of behaviour. The culturally rich home environment tends to pick up the hidden potentials. Creativity blossoms in an atmosphere where the child feels free to take chances and risk and unusual ideas—where he can be playful. It seems to be quite reasonable to think of creative development in the light of one's cultural heritage. This is not rare that even a superficial observation makes it clear that some cultures have rich heritage of customs, ceremonial function and daily life activities which attach strong importance to artistic expressions like dance, music, painting, decoration, drama and other artistic displays. The family in itself is an important unit providing amenities, resources and opportunities for cognitive development within the broader spectrum of cultural environment. With this realization and observation various cross-cultural studies have been conducted to examine the differences, if any, in the creative development which can be attributed to a greater extent to the healthy and enriched cultural constituents. Cross-cultural researches enable us to make more definite and unqualified generalizations about some variables of human behaviour when their occurrence has been confirmed in a cross-cultural research. The ecological status of one place may differentiate it from other parts of a country due to its cultural mode. That is why it is suggested that the study on one cultural group needs to be replicated in areas of other varieties and other culture. Comparative results of such studies will contribute to many good 'clues' to our comprehension and knowledge. Such cross-cultural studies will contribute many precious facts toward understanding of creativity on various dimensions.

In cross-cultural studies individual variation is held constant while variation in the culture is the subject of study. The members composing a culture are treated as homogenous, because it is the typical representative or normative aspect of behaviour of cultural unit that is taken into consideration (Mohsin, S.M., 1984).

Thus, cross-cultural studies, if well-planned and controlled, can provide a better opportunity to isolate creative activites as manifested in a particular culture which encourages and stimulates such activities. Preferences and recognition for creative endeavour and involvement in creative work do influence such behaviour. If studies are conducted on a large sample, the effect of cultural variation may be better recognized by the investigator. Various findings in this framework are available which point towards cultural variation as a factor in the growth of creative potentials. Torrance (1962) conducted a study on a sample of 1000 students from Australia, Germany, U.S., India, Samoa and US whites. His findings reveal that in all cultures, except that of Samoa, the development curves of creative thinking abilities contained discontinuities. The drops occured in Kinder Garten, third, fourth and seventh grades and slight drop at high school level. Thus, the findings pointed towards the similarities of creative performance in all cultures.

Sallery (1968) studied creativity in 48 Arabs and 48 Canadians and found that extraordinary subjects showed greater degree of complexity and details in free hand-drawing in both the cultures. Doyle (1970) in his study on 27 Negroes and 31 Caucasians of seventh and eighth classes, observed Negro subjects to be superior on creativity to Caucasians. However, the statistical significance was not observed in respect of the difference between these two groups. Richmond (1971), compared the performance of Negro and Caucasian school students and found the latter to be better on verbal fluency and flexibility, figural flexibility and originality. The Negroes showed higher scores on figural elaboration.

However, Vernon's (1967) study indicated no marked differences in creative imagination of English, Haleridean, Eskimo (Canadian) and Indian children, though only Indian showed lower originality, which probably could be attributed to lack of cultural stimulation, conservatism and non-cooperation with white civilization. Strauss and Strauss (1968) have found American sample to display higher creativity as compared to Indian sample and argued in favour of this difference due to degree of freedom enjoyed by American population.

Hussain and Hussain (1975) studied a female sample from Aligarh and male from that of Ranchi district which represent two subcultural backgrounds. Significant differences in favour of female on the originality measures were observed, whereas, on fluency, flexibility and elaboration the differences were not found to be significant though upwardly girl's mean scores were higher. These differences have been attributed to cultural variations. The researchers stressed girl's early maturity than that of boys.

These studies on creative abilities of persons from different countries and culture, however, do not clearly support a single trend. In one study subjects from one specific culture are found to be less creative while in other to be more creative. The studies are only relative in relation to situational variables and tests, etc.

In spite of such controversies, cultural influences, in general, have been presumed to facilitate or inhibit the expression of creative potentials present within an individual.

A number of studies are available on socio-economic status as a factor in creative growth and development. It is to be pointed out that SES has been also considered as the main constituent of cultural influences: such findings have been already quoted in the previous section of this book. On the whole, high socioeconomic status of the family has been found to affect positively the expression of creative potentials as it provides better resources and facilities for involvement in creative activities. Members of such family are more enlightened and appreciate diversion and uniqueness.

One thing to be pointed out is that some authors hold the opinion that cross-cultural studies, in true sense, are those which include different cultures from different countries. However, it seems difficult to organize such researches with our limited resources. That is why, in India cross-cultural studies on creativity and intelligence have been generally conducted on the tribal and non-tribal population, who display distinct and separate cultural way of living. Some researchers have even referred to urban and rural differences on the measures of creativity. Sharma (1972) has reported rural subjects to be more creative in comparison to their urban counterparts. The present author, however, feels that in the age of modernity, facilities for transportation, exposure to mass-media communication and other such factors have minimized the cultural variation between the urban and the rural students. Further, the word 'culture' should not be used while referring to urban and rural population of the same region unless marked cultural disparity and uniqueness are observed. As far as the studies on tribal and non-tribal population are concerned, caution must be taken to isolate non-tribal from tribal by studying the urban population of capital cities and non-tribal from remote tribal belts, who still maintain some identity of their cultural heritage. However, it is difficult to claim now that with the increasing technology and advancement in social living the tribals are completely isolated from their non-tribal counterpart and constitute a totally different cultural group. With all such limitations in mind, Hussain, S. (1985) conducted a cross-cultural study on creativity on a sample of tribal and non-tribal population of Bihar. The research paper based on this study was accepted for presentation at Eighth International Congress of Cross-cultural Psychology held at Istanbul, Turkey in July 1986. The details of the study are as follows:

The study was conducted on the two cultural groups with the aim to investigate into the differences, if any, in creative behaviour of these two. The purpose underlying the study was to examine whether socio-cultural heritage contributes to the growth of creative potentials. The customs, rituals, art, ceremonial functions, folkways, etc. of a specific culture may contribute, atleast, to non-verbal creativity. The investigator did not include intelligence as a factor to be interlinked with the study on creativity while investigating into the effect of cultural factors on the creative development. The reason behind this was that the review of the literature on intelligence and creativity suggested that intelligence may be a necessary but not the sufficient condition of creativity. Only minimal level of intelligence may be required for the development of creativity. Further, intelligence and creativity have been found to be independent of each other by a number of investigators, already quoted earlier.

In India a number of tribal communities inhabit Bihar, of them the Mundas, the Oraons and the Santhals constitute, numerically, socially, economically and also politically the major ones. They are concentrated in two parts of Bihar, the Chotanagpur Plateau and Santhal Parganas district, i.e. south and north-eastern parts of Bihar respectively. The Santhals are the largest tribal community of the state in terms of population, and next to them are the Mundas and Oraons. These two communities have led a relatively unmolested life in the Chotanagpur Plateau for centuries before the British annexed the area. (Choudhary, 1977). These tribes are found in different territories of Bihar having their own culture. The tribal communities have maintained their distinct ethnic identity for centuries, although from time to time the tribal culture has been influenced by such alien factors as Hinduism and Christianity. However, they continue to maintain the basic elements of their systems. The tribal people have marked aesthetic sense which is revealed in the manner they erect mud-coloured wall of their houses and paint on them with pitcher of flowers, creepers, etc.

in a simple way. Their love for music and dance is well known. They play a variety of unsophisticated musical instrument. The festivals and the marriages are organized in highly artistic way. On the whole, the dancing, singing, painting and decoration reflect the basic core of the cultural heritage of tribal people.

The Chotanagpur Plateau inhabited by tribal people has so far been a paradise for researches by anthropologists. Numerous anthropological studies are available to date but researches by psychologists are negligible in comparison to the former; specially no attempt has been made to study the creativity of tribals and compare it with that of non-tribal subjects. It was to fill this gap that the present research was conceived and conducted. The tribal and non-tribal people of Bihar, belonging to Ranchi and Patna district respectively, were selected for the present investigation. The conceptualization underlying the present study was that if cultural stimulation and heritage contribute to the growth of creative potentials the tribal people would do better on test of creativity, especially of non-verbal nature, as compared to their non-tribal counterparts.

METHOD

Sample

The sample consisted of 320 tribal and non-tribal male and female school students.

The method of incidental sampling was applied in selecting the sample for study. The sex differences were taken into consideration for studying creativity, as the present researcher himself in collboration with Sajid S.M. (1984) found that the male and female respondents differed significantly on their scores on test of divergent thinking. Various other researchers have also quoted the role of sex variance in creative behaviour (Solomon, 1968; Bowers, 1971; Goyal, 1973; Kogen, 1974; Yamamoto 1960; Torrance, 1965; Fletcher 1968; Neufeld, 1964; Rajik, 1964; Hussain and Hussain, 1975).

The scheme for the sampling emerged as follows :

N = 320

Tribals (N = 160) — Non-Tribals (N = 160)

Male (N = 80) Female (N = 80) Male (N = 80) Female (N = 80)

Measures

For the measurement of non-verbal creativity the test of non-verbal divergent thinking (Mehdi, B. 1973) was used. This test intends to measure the individual's ability to deal with figural content in a creative manner by using activities like picture completion of triangles and ellipses. The test measures divergent thinking in terms of elaboration, originality and also yields composite scores. The rationale behind measuring only the non-verbal creativity was that the tribal people might not be well versed on verbal items as compared to their non-tribal counterparts.

Procedure

The test of non-verbal divergent thinking was administered to the selected sample of 320 tribal and non-tribal male and female school students in small groups to secure their full attention and cooperation. Two sets of responses from tribal and non-tribal subjects were obtained, scored, tabulated and finally analysed by applying t-test in order to find out whether the two groups differed significantly on their mean scores on non-verbal creativity.

RESULTS AND DISCUSSION

Comparisons of tribal and non-tribal subjects were made on the basis of their scores on the test of non-verbal divergent thinking. The purpose was to examine whether the two cultural groups differed significantly in terms of their creativity. Their mean scores on the test of non-verbal divergent thinking were compared and the 't' values were found out. The two groups were compared on their scores on elaboration, and originality aspects as well as on their composite scores. The scheme for the comparison was as follows :

(a) Tribal versus non-tribal male students
(b) Tribal versus non-tribal female students
(c) Tribal male versus female students
(d) Non-tribal male versus female students

The findings are given in Table 4.1 and 4.2 along with their interpretation.

TABLE 4.1: **Mean Scores of Tribal and non-Tribal Male Subjects on non-Verbal Test of Divergent Thinking along with SD and 't' Values**

	Groups	*N*	*Mean*	*SD*	*SE*	*df*	*t-value*	*Significance level*
Elaboration	Tribal males	80	88.69	24.44	2.73	158	3.08	.01
	Non-Tribal males	80	77.80	20.15	2.25			
Originality	Tribal males	80	20.86	7.68	.86	158	10.70	.01
	Non-tribal males	80	48.90	22.14	2.18			
Composite Scores	Tribal Males	80	109.54	28.62	3.20	158	2.90	.01
	Non-tribal Males	80	125.00	38.28	4.28			

The analysis of the results in table 4.1 indicates that the tribal male subjects are superior to their non-tribal counterparts on the elaboration aspect of divergent thinking only ($P<.01$) whereas, the non-tribals have an edge over the tribals in respect of their mean scores on originality aspect as well as on composite mean scores (P<.01). Thus on the whole, the non-tribal male subjects have been observed to be more creative in comparison to tribal male subjects.

TABLE: 4.2 **Mean scores of tribal and non-tribal female subjects on non-verbal test of divergent thinking along with SD, SE and 't' values**

	Groups	*N*	*Mean*	*SD*	*SE*	*df*	*t-value*	*Significance level*
Elaboration	Tribal Females	80	86.98	36.44	4.08	158	2.04	.05
	Non-tribal Females	80	77.20	36.52	4.09			
Originality	Tribal Females	80	13.82	4.80	.54	158	3.68	.01
	Non-tribal Females	80	19.85	13.95	1.56			
Composite soores	Tribal Females	80	102.93	26.29	2.94	158	.71	(Not Significant)
	Non-tribal Females	80	100.00	26.00	9.91			

The findings given in table 4.2 indicate a comparative estimate of tribal and non-tribal female subjects on non-verbal divergent thinking. The tribal female subjects have been found to be better on elaboration aspect of divergent thinking (P<.05), whereas the non-tribal subjects have an edge over their tribal counterparts as far as the scores an the originality aspect of divergent thinking are concerned (P<.01). Upwardly the tribal female subjects also seem to have an edge over their non-tribal counterparts with regard to their mean composite scores obtained on the test. However, the mean difference is not statistically significant even at .05 level of confidence, hence nothing definite can be remarked in this direction.

The overall picture that emerged from the findings of Table 4.1 and 4.2 with regard to creativity of tribal and non-tribal male and female subjects suggests that both the tribal males and females are superior on elaboration aspect of non-verbal creativity as compared to their non-tribal counterparts.

As far as the performance on originality aspect of non-verbal creativity is concerned the non-tribal male and female respondents have been found to be superior in comparison to their tribal counterparts. The non-tribal male respondents have been found to be better on their mean composite scores in comparison to their tribal counterparts (125.00 and 109.54 respectively). However, the tribal and non-tribal female subjects have not been found to differ significantly on their mean composite scores obtained on non-verbal test of creativity. Thus, the non-tribal male subjects have displayed better performance on non-verbal creativity test with regard to originality and composite scores, whereas, the tribals have an edge over non-tribals only on elaboration aspect of creativity.

As far as the comparisons of tribal and non-tribal female subjects are exclusively concerned, it has not been possible to show the superiority of one over other. The tribal group is more creative on elaboration aspect whereas non-tribal on the originality aspect. As far as the difference on mean composite scores is concerned it is statistically not significant.

On the whole, the non-tribal subjects have been found to be better on their performance on the test of divergent thinking.

Thus, the findings in respect of the relative performance of tribal and non-tribal male and female subjects both, on the non-verbal test of divergent thinking (Table 4.1 and 4.2), indicate that the conceptualization underlying the present study has not been fully supported by the present researcher. The conceptualization underlying the present study was that the tribal subjects would do better on the test of non-verbal creativity because of their cultural heritage and preoccupation with different creative arts and ceremonial functions. But the findings have shown that the tribal male and female subjects both are superior to their non-tribal counterparts only on one dimension of non-verbal creativity, i.e. elaboration. Thus, the findings are not in the expected direction. The findings may be explained on the rationale that the tribal population is now not completely unmolested as it is exposed to aculturalization. The tribal way of life, consisting of traditional rituals and customs has undergone a significant change after independance. Spread of education, economic development and various other schemes for raising the socio-economic status of tribals have brought changes in the traditional ways of their living. The opening of community development blocks, introduction of integrated rural development programme, improvement in mode of communication and transportation, linking the interior villages with the towns and the expansion of industrial belt around the city have been very much responsible for exposing the tribal communities in Chotanagpur Division to modernization. This exposer to changing patterns and way of life has produced a marked rapid transformation in the behaviour patterns of these tribal people. Contacts with Hinduism, Christianity and various welfare schemes have resulted in revolutionary changes among tribals during last two decades. Vidayarthi (1968) has rightly remarked that changes in religion, the local aspect of culture, brought corresponding changes in festivals, economic life and other overall aspect of tribal culture. The tribal people have undergone selective aculturation. Even the traditional self concept has undergone change by the socialization and training process of the child. Vidayarthi states that a new type of personality has emerged which is different from that of the Sarna Oraon.

The present author conducted his study on the school-going students who come across to the mode of living and thinking of the urban population. It seems quite difficult to have a sample of tribal people which exclusively maintains its original cultural ways of life and practices even today. On the other hand, the non-tribals are now much more exposed to various artistic activities, creative games, hobbies and stimulation provided by the family, school and mass media educational programmes. The urban population now seems to enjoy much more challenging and stimulating environment which is conducive to the growth of creative potentials. Further, it can be said that the non-verbal creativity may not be exclusively determined by one's own culture but by various other factors like socio-economic status, inspiring and encouraging home and school environment, personalistic variables as well as other cognitive factors. So further researches are needed along this direction in order to provide some concrete estimate of cultural influence on the creative behaviour of individuals in our own set-up.

TABLE 4.3: **Mean Scores of Tribal Male and Female Subjects on non-Verbal Test of Divergent Thinking along with SD, SE and 't' Values**

	Groups	*N*	*Mean*	*SD*	*SE*	*df*	*t-value*	*Significance level*
Elaboration	Tribal males	80	88.69	24.44	2.73	158	.06	NS
	Tribal females	80	88.98	36.44	4.08			
Originality	Tribal males	80	20.86	7.68	0.86	158	6.97	.01
	Tribal Females	80	13.82	4.80	0.54			
Composite scores	Tribal Males	80	109.54	28.02	3.14	158	1.54	.05
	Tribal Females	80	102.93	26.29	2.94			

The findings of Table 4.3 suggest the superiority of male tribal subjects over their female counterparts on the originality aspect as well as on the composite scores ($P < .01$ and .05). As far as elaboration aspect of divergent thinking is concerned the difference between the two sexes is not significant.

TABLE 4.4 : **Mean Scores of non-Tribal Male and Female Subjects on the non-Verbal Test of Divergent Thinking along with SD and their 't' values**

	Groups	*N*	*Mean*	*SD*	*SE*	*df*	*t-value*	*Significance level*
Elaboration	Non-tribal males	80	77.80	20.15	2.25	158	.13	NS
	Non-tribal females	80	77.20	36.52	4.09			
Originality	Non-tribal males	80	48.90	22.14	2.48	158	9.95	.01
	Non-tribal females	80	19.85	13.95	1.56			
Composite scores	Non-tribal males	80	125.00	38.28	1.28	158	4.84	.01
	Non-tribal females	80	100.00	26.00	2.91			

The study of Table 4.4 points towards the fact that on elaboration aspect of creativity the non-tribal male and female subjects do not differ significantly ($P>.05$). However, the non-tribal male subjects are superior to their female counterparts on the originality aspect of creativity and also on their composite scores ($P<.01$).

The overall picture of Table 4.3 and 4.4 suggests that male respondents both of tribal and non-tribal communities are superior to their female counterparts on originality as well as on the mean composite scores. Further, it has been noted that the differences between these two groups in respect of their mean scores on elaboration are not significant. This clearly indicates that male respondents are better on non-verbal creativity, in general, as compared to their female counterparts.

This intra-group comparison on the basis of sex differences indicates that sex variance plays a significant role in determining creativity of an individual. Male subjects have been found to be more creative in comparison to their female counterparts, irrespective of cultural variation. The present findings in respect of the superiority of male over female get support from various other research findings:

Strauss and Strauss (1968) making a wider cross-cultural study, observed clear-cut sex differences in American and Indian student populations. In both the societies, boys were significantly high creatives than girls. They further explored that the gaps were wider in Indians than Americans. Probably this may be due to the degree of cultural and social advancement in America.

Kelly (1965) on a sample of fourth grade students, found that boys were observed significantly more creative than girls on non-verbal creativity measures.

Prakash (1966) studying fourth grade Indian Children found boys to be significantly high creative than the girls. Similar results on Indian students have been reported by Raina (1968, 1969). He pointed that the Indian girls face many restrictions in family and society and find no opportunity for free expression of their ideas and views.

Another Indian study of high school students also supports the boy's superiority over girls in respect of creativity (Gagneja, (1972), Mar'l, S.K. (1971) in his study on Arab rural Ss of eight grade, observed significantly high creativity scores in favour of males over females on nine scores out of thirteen, drawn from the battery of Torrance Tests of creative thinking.

On a college sample of 191 females and 123 males, Middents (1968) found boy's scores significantly higher than those of girls on elaboration aspect of non-verbal creativity. In one study the U.S. boys had also been found significantly high on most of the measures of verbal originality (Torrance, 1962, 1965; Torrance and Aliotti, 1969) as well as on figural originality (Dhir, 1973), semantic flexibility (Guilford, 1964) and total flexibility (Hardlow, 1967) than what girls had scored. Sajid, S.M. (1984) also found that school-going boys were superior to girls on non-verbal creativity.

The above findings suggest that boys are more creative than

girls. Though some of the studies point out cultural and social restrictions imposed upon girls as the cause of their creativity, yet it seems, much is to be explored as to what are the reasons of this low creativity in girls. Kogan (1974), surveying the literature on sex differences, concluded that the greater susceptibility of women to distractions related to social context which handicap their creative achievements. The cognitive, conative and affective factors should also be taken into consideration for having correct picture of the event.

Another important cross-cultural study on the tribal and non-tribal population of Bihar, was conducted by De, B. (1984). He studied cognitive style and cognitive ability of tribal and non-tribal high school population. The investigator attempted to investigate, in a cross-cultural setting, the empirical validity of cognitive style and its educational significance. He also included creative thinking and intelligence as cognitive variables. Cognitive style refers to the characteristic way in which individuals conceptually organize their perception. Two such ways are 'field dependent' and 'field independent'. The purpose of this study was to investigate whether the tribal students studying in high school would differ from their non-tribal counterparts on the field dependence-field independence dimension and whether this dimension bore any significant relationship with intelligence and creativity. The specific purpose was to find out if cognitive style was related to reasoning and creative thinking. The sample consisted of the Oraon and Munda students reading in high school, having age range of 12-14 years. Both Christian and non-Christians (Sarna) male and female students were included in the tribal group. Similarly the non-tribal group consisted of high caste as well as schedule caste Hindu male and female students. The size of sample in each category was 20. The tools used for the study were Witkin's embedded figure test for measuring cognitive style; Raven's progressive matrices test of general intelligence and Mehdi's non-verbal creative thinking test. The results were analysed by using statistical techniques like Mann-Whitney U test and co-efficient of concordance test. The first technique was to test the significance of difference between the mean scores on the three cognitive variables whereas the second technique was applied to determine the relationship, if any, among these three variables. The findings of this study, specially with regard to creativity are as follows: Neither the male nor the female tribals significantly differed from their non-tribal counterparts.

In respect of the tribal sub-groups, the Oraon male Christian and Sarna students showed no significant difference, however, their female counterparts did at .01 level of confidence, the means of the female Christian and Sarna students being 118.5 and 96.5 respectively. In the case of Munda male students no significant difference was found between the mean scores of Christian and sarna students, but the means of their female counterparts differed significantly at .05 level of confidence; the means of Christian female and those of sarna counterparts were 109.5 and 88.5 respectively. Thus, the Christian female respondents, both Oraon and Mundas were observed to be superior in creative thinking in comparison to their Sarna counterparts. The findings regarding the high caste and low caste male and female students indicated that the male students did not differ significantly on the mean scores on test of creativity, whereas the female respondents differed at .05 level of confidence.

Further, the findings based on the application of Kendall's coefficient of concordance, yielded the nature of association among the three variables. A positive and substantial association was observed among the three variables in tribal male and female subjects. It was found that those people whose cognitive style involves the least censoring of the information available in the external world are most likely to be creative thinkers.

However, this finding is to be further tested. While commenting upon the research findings, De, B. himself has cautioned against the generalized inferences to be made on the ground that the size of the sample was not large and further the samples were taken from the urban population. The urbanization might have resulted in greater acculturation of the tribal population. Hence, further efforts are to be made in this direction.

Thus, in the light of above quoted empirical studies one can well appreciate the fact that researches on creativity should also be conducted in cross-cultural perspective. This step would help in analyzing the various components of culture as they contribute to creativity of an individual. Studies on creativity in relation to intelligence and other cognitive abilities, sex, familial background, socio-economic status and personalistic variables should be conducted in a cross-cultural framework. This will help in locating the contribution of various cognitive and non-cognitive correlates of creativity, taking cultural environment into consideration. The present author, thus, recommends further extensive researches on creativity in a cross-cultural perspective.

A comparative picture emerging from cross-cultural findings will enhance our knowledge in respect of the expression of creative potentials. This will further help in analyzing the restraint imposed by the culture and its adverse effects on the expression of creativity of its members.

CHAPTER FIVE

PERSONALITY CHARACTERISTICS AND CREATIVITY

Creativity has been generally explained in the light of cognitive abilities of an individual. Intelligence and divergent thinking have been given due importance by the investigators and this much can be atleast said that the main stream of research has been along this direction. However, the readers must recognize, in the light of early discussion, that only cognitive variables are not to be associated with creativity rather personality characteristics do have their impact on the creative performance. Empirical researches have also been conducted to support this notion. The question arises whether there is anything special about creative people in addition to their creativity and the tendency to make good use of divergent thinking? Do they have certain personality traits in common which contribute to creative activities? This approach deals with the explication of personality characteristics in determining the creative development.

It is presumed that creative individuals exhibit higher sensitivity, aesthetic sense, independent judgement and thinking, initiative and preference for perceptual novelty and multiplexity. Many other characteristics have been also noted in this context. The study of such personality characteristics may be linked with the study of personality trait theory of creativity. This theory emphasized the exploration of traits which a creative individual possesses. This theory emerged out of various research findings related to creative individuals in the light of their personality traits. Mainly the exploration of traits of the professional creative artists or scientists has been made.

Cattell and Drevdahl (1955) compared the scores of 140 eminent research scientists in American universities, tested with Cattell's 16 PF questionnaire, with those of university teachers and administrators and also with the average score of the general population. The research scientists and the presumably less creative university group showed fairly a resemblance in personality profile, compared with the general population norms, but interesting differences were also found. The research scientists were found to be more withdrawn and unsociable, less emotionally stable, more intellectually self-sufficient and more radical. The same differences were found when Drevdahl (1956) compared creative and non-creative students in science and arts subjects.

Cross, Cattell and Butcher (1967) have observed that the 16 PF clearly brings distinction between artists (art teachers and professional painters) and a controlled group matched for age and level of education. The artist differed significantly on 12 out of 15 factors (intelligence excluded) particularly in being more dominant and intellectually self-sufficient but lower on ego strength and consciousness.

Cattell (1963) reviewed the evidence about scientists of genius and observed that their level of ego strength and emotional stability was certainly higher than the average of the general population. While referring to Kretschmer's observation, he supported his version that there was presence of high anxiety in many creative people. There are evidences of high anxiety level in productive researchers. Some have reported high rate of neurosis and psychosis among artists, writers and composers. Some of the high creative genius have been found to have alter-ego and disturbing auditory hallucination.

There is some evidence that creative persons are more autonomous than others, more self-sufficient, more independent in judgement, more open to the irrational in themselves; more stable, feminine in interest and characteristics, dominant and self-assertive, complex, self-accepting, resourceful, adventurous, radical, self-controlled and more emotionally sensitive and introverted (Butcher, J., 1970).

Creative scientists have been found to rate themselves high in professional self-confidence, self-sufficiency, independence and emotional restraint and low in aggressiveness, assertion, social desirability, sociability and masculine vigour (Butcher, J., 1970).

Barron (1963) quotes some experiments on independence of judgement and associated features of personality having relevance to creativity. He found that usually about 25% of subjects stick firmly to their own opinion while about 75% agree with what is held by majority. Barron found that the 'independents' rated themselves significantly more often as artistic, 'emotional' and 'original'. These three qualities brought differences between the self-ratings of the 'independents' and the 'yielders'.

Creative persons have been observed to be less concerned about what others think of them and feel free to let their thinking range over a wide field of possibilities including some that are taboo, and to put forward original ideas.

Dellas and Gaier (1970) have shown that interests, attitudes and desires seem to be more consistent predictors of creativity than is intelligence.

Munsterberg and Mussen, 1953; Eiduson, 1958; Barron, 1962; Taft, 1961; Prados, 1944; Drevdahl and Cattell, 1958; Mackinnon, 1961; Roe, 1952, etc., have studied painters, writers, artists architects and creative scientists. In these researches, measures like personality and temperament questionnaire, rating and personal blanks were used. However, Torrance (1962) is highly credited for compiling all such studies and enlisting 84 personality traits which are quite relevant to creative individuals. Sharma K.N. (1979) has also referred these characteristics in his book on creativity. Some of these characteristics are as follows:

Liking for adventure, altruism, awareness of others, attraction toward disorder, attraction towards mysteries; attempting at difficult jobs, constructive in criticism, courageous, defiance of conventions of courtesy, desire to excel, determination, differentiated value hierarchy, discontented, dominance, emotional, emotional sensitiveness, energetic, versatile, willing to take risk, withdrawn and quiscent, fault finder, doesn't fear being thought different, full of curiosity, likes solitude, independent in judgement, independent in thinking, individualistic, intuitive, industrious, introversive, non-conforming, not hostile or negativistic, not popular, oddities of habit, persistent, preoccupied with a problem, prefers complex ideas, questioning, radical, receptive to external stimuli, receptive to ideas of others, rejection of suppression as a mechanism of impulse control, reserved, resolute, self-assertive, self-starter, self-aware, self-confident, self-sufficient, sensitive to beauty, sincere, not interested in small details, speculative, spirited in disagreement, strives for distant goals, temperamental, tenacious, thorough, unconcerned about power, somewhat uncultured, primitive, unsophisticated, naive, unwilling to accept anything on mere say on.

Further, tolerance for disorder and ambiguity; independence of judgement and uniqueness of ideas are also needed on the part of the individual who are exhibiting creative talents.

Comparative studies are also available on artists–non-artists, and scientists–non-scientists. Personality factors like stability, anxiety, neuroticism and emotional stability, dominance, independence of emotional behaviour, sensitivity towards others, unconventionality and flexibility, originality, ego involvement and ego strength, control over the impulses, early interest in intellectual activities and hobbies and emotional responsiveness have been comparatively observed to be present in creative individuals (Roger and McGruire, 1967; Cattell, 1963; Eiduson, 1962; Taylor and Barron, 1963; Cattell, 1958; Butcher, 1970).

Some studies on creative artists have indicated that creative individuals show introversion and have strong guilt feeling; they have greater exhibitionistic tendency, curiosity and drive toward self-prestige and recognition. Some investigations have shown these artists in different form. They have been observed to be gloomy, bitter, cool, unstable, pessimist and pleasure-seeking (Barron, 1969). Characteristics like need for achievement, passivity and abstract thinking, have been also reported. Hammer (1961) has reported the presence of such characteristics as confidence, determination, independence, rebelliousness, emotionality and behavioural retreat. Drevdahl (1956) observed creativity to be associated with verbal fluency, flexibility, withdrawal, radicalism non-conformity and emotional sensitivity. Some have reported need for achievement and dominance as the characteristics of creative individuals.

Munsterberg and Mussen (1953) have observed artists to be introverted and having a strong guilt-feeling, and displaying less overt aggressive behaviour. However, the need for expression as the acceptance of their work was considered to be more important than material gain.

Bhattacharia (1956) conducted a study and found that creatives possess shallow feelings for life, high sensitivity and ability for prelogical thinking. Further, the researcher observed that persons belonging to the group of born creatives, as he classified, shown greater introversion whereas those belonging to acquired creative group exhibited greater extraversion. Freud remarked that the artist is an incipient introvert who is not far from being neurotic. Taft (1961) found introversion along with originality, action, idealism in higher degrees in creative actors.

Cattell and John (1964) found creativity to be much more associated with emotional stability.

Drevdahl (1964) observed fewer signs of neuroticism in the early life of creative and non-productive creative groups in comparison to the non-creative, non-productive group. Kurtzman, *et al.* (1967) have observed creative adolescent, in their study, to be adventurous, extroverted and self confident in comparison to their non-creative-counterparts. Litle John (1967) has also shown that creative girls did not exhibit any neurotic deviation.

Board, *et al.* (1971) have observed creative individuals to be extroverted.

Cacha (1971) has found creatives to be happy-go-lucky, socially bold and relaxed.

Bhattacharya (1960) studied the personality characteristics of some renowned painters of India and isolated the following characteristics of them as a group.

Intelligence, constructive capacities, relative ideas of form and depth, perception of chromatic values and achromatic shades, verbal acquiety, confidence, sociability, spontaneity, eccentricity and absorbing nature.

Ahmad (1969) conducted a study on 150 female school students in order to explore some of the personality dimensions associated with creativity, The subjects were divided into high 20% and low 20% on the basis of the composite scores of the 3 tests of originality. The high and low creative groups were compared on six personality traits: activity, attempt to moral values, dominance, depression, introversion and emotional stability. The findings, however, indicated that the two groups only differed on dominance significantly. The originals were thus, found to be more dominant than the non-originals.

Raina (1968) investigated into the personality correlates of creativity on a sample of students of Rajasthan (N=500). He found a positive correlation but not significant between creativity and intelligence. However, he observed a significant differences of IQ between the high and low creative groups.

Goyal (1974) conducted a study on personality and creativity by using a sample of middle school stage children of Punjab. He measured creativity on his own test. He found that creative children showed a higher level of energy, rejected repression and supression, were more introverts, were more independent in thought and action, had open mind and could tolerate ambiguity and entertain opposing values.

Pathak (1969), while studying the sample of 200 male and female school-going students of New Delhi, found non-significant relationship between creativity and introversion.

Joshi (1974), in his study on creativity and personality traits of the intellectually gifted high school students found non-significant relationship between creativity scores and different personality traits.

Upadhyaya (1977), found creative group to be more intelligent and socially bold, less tense and having a stronger self sentiment than the low creative group.

Hassan, Q. and Khan, S.R. (1976) have reported in their research findings that fluency scores on test of creativity were found to be significantly correlated with six dimensions of personality traits: sociable, active, cheerful, placid, impulsive and ascendent. All the correlational values were significant at ·01 level, except that of creativity and ascendence. Further, scores on flexibility aspect of creativity were reported to be correlated with five dimensions of temperament: active, sociable, placid, reflective and tough-minded. The co-efficients of correlation were significant at ·01 level in the case of first three and at ·05 level in the case of last two dimensions of temperament. 'Originality', as a strand of creativity, only correlated with two dimensions of temperament: 'reflective' and 'active'. The significance level was ·05. 'Activity' was the only dimension of temperament which was significantly correlated with fluency, flexibility and originality scores.

Chauhan, 1977; Srivastava, 1978; Gulati, 1979; Verma, 1979 and Kumar, 1981 have found creativity to have positive and significant correlation with introversion. Nagia (1977) and Bhargava (1979) have reported negative correlation between extraversion and creativity scores.

Jarial, 1980; and Jarial and Sharma, 1981 have observed a non-significant differcnce between introverts and extroverts on fluency, flexibility and originality components of creativity.

Jarial and Verma (1979) reported creatives to be more intelligent, enthusiastic, adaptable, relaxed, outgoing, warm-hearted, participating, self-controlled, self-disciplined and preferring own decision.

Lal, Ramjee (1986) made a projective study of personality dynamics of creative adolescents. The study aimed to investigate the differences between the needs, as conceptualized by Murray, of creative and non-creative adolescents. The sample for the present study consisted of 150 male adolescents studying in the colleges of Deoria district (U.P). The subjects were within the age range of 17–20 years. For the measurement of creativity, the creativity instrument devised by Wallach and Kogan (1965) and adapted by Paramesh (1969) were selected and used after translating the verbal part of the test into Hindi. For the assessment of personality dynamics of high and low creative adolescents, the Indian adaptation of Thematic Apperception Test by Bureau of Psychology, Allahabad was used. The obtained data were subjected to inferential statistical analysis. To ascertain the nature and amount of relationship between different psychogenic needs and creativity, the phi-coefficient correlation values were tested against the null-hypothesis by applying the chi-square test.

The results of the present study reveal that high and low creative groups differ significantly in respect of eight psychogenic needs, viz. n ach, n def, n abase, n auto, n aggr, n dom, n nurtu, and n succ. It is evident from the analysis of results that high creatives accomplish something difficult. They manipulate or organize physical objects, human beings or ideas rapidly and as independently as possible. They overcome obstacles and attain a high standard. High creative adolescents try to increase self regard by the successful exercise of talent. Exhibiting the need for autonomy, high creative resists coercion and restriction. They avoid activities prescribed by domineering authorities. They try to be independent and free to act according to impulse. They also want to be unattached, unconditioned and irresponsible. The other chief characteristics of high creative adolescents showing need for aggression are their efforts to overcome opposition forcefully, to fight, to revenge an injury, to belittle, censure and to influence or direct the behaviour of organisms by suggestion, seduction, persuation, or command. They want to be nursed, supported, sustained, surrounded, protected, loved, advised, guided, indulged, forgiven and consoled. They do not conform to custom. They do not admit inferiority, error, wrong-doing or defeat.

Pandey, M.S. (1986) studied motivational determinants of creativity. In this study the role of achievement motivation and risk-taking in creativity was examined on a sample of 400 school children in the State of Bihar. The criterion variable had been measured by Wallach Kogan (1965) battery of creativity instrument as adapted by Sharma (1976). Predicting variables were measured by Bhatia Achievement motivation test and by Kogan wallach (1964) choiced dialema questionnare (risk-taking). Inconsistent results were obtained in case of the male and female group. Achievement motivation failed to differentiate the high and the low creatives in males as well as in females. However, the risk-taking differentiated the high and low male creatives.

Gakhar and Joshi (1980) found highly fluent and flexible respondents to be characterized by greater socialization whereas highly original respondents by greater self-acceptance, responsibility, stability, emotional balance, self sufficiency, dominance, self confidence and extraversion.

Haber, R.N. and Fried, H.A. (1975) have also mentioned some personality characteristics of creative people, which are based on the data yielded on personality inventories. The creative people tend to be more individualistic, inventive, artistic, persevering, open-minded, self-perceptive and emotional than rest of the population. While these characteristics cannot always be used to differentiate between creative and non-creative people, they seem to be more frequent among the former.

In the light of the controversial findings with regard to the type of relationship of extraversion/introversion and neuroticism with creativity, Sharan, P. under the supervision of Hussain, S. (1986), conducted an extensive study on the population of the state of Bihar. For measuring extraversion, introversion and neuroticism Hindi adaptation of Eysenck's Moudsly personality inventory (Jalota, S. and Kapoor, S.D.) was used, whereas verbal and non-verbal creativity was assessed by Mehdi test of creativity, (Mehdi, B.). The sample consisted of 400 male and female students. The findings showed that high creatives differed significantly from their low counterparts on the mean scores obtained on neuroticism scale. The obtained mean values of high creative on both verbal and non-verbal tests were reported to be 12·51 and 15·19, whereas that of low creatives to be 22·55 and 25·36, respectively, having $P < \cdot 01$. The higher scores on neuroticism scale indicated higher neurotic tendency. Thus, the high creative groups were observed to have lesser neurotic tendencies as compared to low creatives. The argument which has been extended in support of this finding was that the neurotics are commonly not highly creatives as they are touchy, anxious and restless which may affect creativity adversely. The findings were further supported by the correlational results and multiple regression analysis which indicated that neuroticism is negatively correlated with creativity and it does not contribute to creativity positively, various findings have been already quoted earlier which extend support to the findings of Sharan, P.

Further, Sharan, P. investigated into the relationship of

creativity to extraversion/introversion as it was observed to be highly controversial issess. She has given a detailed account of various characterizing features of extroverts and introverts. While defining such concepts the researcher presented views of Jung and Eysenck. Eysenck who made a factorial analysis of the personality traits characterizing introversion and extraversion in terms of tridimensional theory, states that a typical extrovert is sociable, enjoys parties, has a number of friends, likes people to talk to him, craves for excitement and stimulation, takes chances, acts on the spur of the moment and likes change. He is carefree, optimist, easy-going and prefers to keep moving and doing things. On the other hand, a typical introvert appears to be quiet, retiring, reserved and indifferent, very cautious and does not like excitement. He takes up any matter with proper seriousness and shows aggressive behaviour seldom. He has pessimistic outlook and conforms to the ethical standards. However, it is difficult to have such a perfect extrovert or introvert in real life. The majority of people seem to occupy a position in between these two.

In the present research of Sharan, P. extraversion–introversion were measured by Hindi adaptation of Moudsley personality inventory. Creativity was assessed by Mehdi Verbal and Non-verbal tests of creativity. The findings indicated that high scorers on verbal and non-verbal creativity both obtained greater mean scores on extraversion as compared to their low counterparts. The difference between the two means was also significant at ·01 level. The findings thus suggested that respondents higher on creativity scores showed greater extraversion. However, by applying regression analysis technique the researcher observed a positive but non-significant individual contribution of extraversion to creativity. Thus, the findings of Sharan, P. is again indecisive, however, partially lend support to the assumption that persons higher on creativity exhibit greater extraversion qualities. On the whole, the characteristics of creative people have many qualities of an extrovert (Runner, *et al.*, 1954). These important behaviour patterns are characterized by seeking change and adventure, paying attention to things important to one's own self, awaiting development and change in the plan quickly, questioning rules and authority, being tolerant, and open-minded, acting impulsively and not sticking to a single course of action. Various empirical findings have been already quoted earlier in support of the positive relationship between creativity and extraversion.

The investigator further made a comprehensive study of creativity in relation to adjustment of an individual. While planning the study she mainly concentrated on the conceptual framework developed by Hussain, S. (1985) with regard to adjustment, of course, some other views were also incorporated. Amidst various controversies regarding an agreed definition of adjustment she followed the following interpretation given by Hussain, S. Adjustment can be regarded as a process by which the individual tries his best to maintain a harmonious, stable and satisfying relationship with his environment. In the process of adjustment an individual attempts at satisfying his needs in the light of environmental pressure as well as his own abilities and limitations. A healthy adjustment aims at long term satisfaction instead of satisfying an immediate need. Thus, while analyzing adjustment one should try to look into the ways by which individuals respond to the demands of their environment as well as satisfaction of their own motives. Further, one should remember that it is difficult to describe people as well adjusted or poorly adjusted because adjustment involves a continuous variable.

Kaplan (1965) has rightly remarked that standards of adjustive behaviour pattern vary with time, place, culture, circumstances and the individual characteristics. Criteria against which adjustment is evaluated either as good or bad are provided by a specific cultural framework, based on its value system which goes on changing from one culture to another and from one generation to other. It is better to judge individual as adjusted or maladjusted in terms of how well he modifies himself in the light of the demands that he encounters. This capacity again varies with the human developmental level. Thus, it seems more appropriate to evaluate adjustment in terms of a person's capability to encounter with the problems appropriate to his developmental level. In short, it is difficult to obtain a single yardstick against which an individual's adjustment can be judged as healthy or poor. However, some general and overall characteristics of a well adjusted person have been enumerated by Hussain, S. A well adjusted person maintains a stable, harmonious and satisfying relationship with his environment. He satisfies his needs within the available resources. While satisfying his needs he takes into consideration his own welfare as well as that of others. His perception is reality based, as he is aware of his assets and limitations both. He exercises control over his impulses, thoughts, habits, emotion and behaviour at large. He is more or less free from depression, intense fear, morbid anxieties, hostile tendencies, guilt feeling, insecurity and disruption of thought. In short, his behaviour is neither disturbing to himself nor to the society. In this continuation Telford's (1971) conception of the 6 dimensions of adjustment are also worth noting. These dimensions include selective awareness, tolerance, autonomy, personal integration, self-esteem and self-realization. Keeping in view these six dimensions, one can observe that adequate adjustment selectively helps in distinguishing between the relevant and irrelevant thoughts. A high level of attentive concentration on significant problems needs selective awareness which helps an individual in distinguishing the real from the spurious and the fake from the genuine. This selective awareness has been also referred to as liberty to focus on main purpose which comprises an important component of adjustment.

Further, a well-adjusted person has a tolerance for his own shortcomings and also strives for improvement. However, he remains to be problem-centred and is not very much defensive in his motivation. He does not develop unproductive anxiety over the discrepancy between his real self and the ideal self. He accepts other people. He finds the world a pretty good place which is worth living, but also considers that it still needs improvement.

As far as autonomy is concerned, it is stressed that over conformity or non-conformity both are handicapping and maladaptive. The compulsive non-conformist lacks freedom, flexibility, rationality and adaptibility although he usually perceives himself as free, independent, original and creative.

As far as personal integration is concerned Telford and his associates have remarked that to be productively creative requires a certain loosness in one's personality structure. It involves the interaction of facts with fantacies and a capacity for perceiving the fimiliar in new ways. It appears that individuals having personal integration possess creative potentials.

With regard to self-esteem as component of adjustment, it has been said what a person believes about himself constitutes a kind of internal cognitive map for living.

Self-realization or self-actualization as a component of adjustment may have its significant role in constructive works. The individual is considered to realize his potentials and this realization is a positive, constructive and realistic process, Rogers (1961). Self-realization cannot consist in achieving a fixed goal rather deriving satisfaction from personally and socially valued directions.

These various aspects of human adjustment motivated the investigator, Sharan, P. to study adjustment in relation to creativity. The argument in favour of such studies can be that a better adjustment may have its facilitating effect on the development of creative activities. However, one can also argue against it on the ground that even a schizophrenic can produce creative paintings and writings. Of course, their analysis may reveal underlying anxiety, conflicts, strivings, emotionality as well as fantasies.

As far as the existing empirical findings are concerned in respect of adjustment and creativity, they are controversial. some have reported healthy adjustment to be facilitating to creativity whereas others emphasized poor adjustment for creative output. Drevdahl (1964) stressed superior personal, social and emotional adjustment of creative groups.

Goyal (1974), while studying creative science students found that they were characterized by higher level of intelligence, emotional stability and better adjustment. Singh, R. (1975) indicated in his findings that various components of creativity showed positive and significant relationship with emotional adjustment as well as with social adjustment.

Gupta, *et al.*, (1976) found creativity to have positive and significant relation with social, emotional and educational adjustment of the individual. Babu, N. (1977) studied the adjustment of those respondents who scored high on creativity and intelligence measures and observed this group to exhibit group adjustment as well as individual adjustment.

Singh, R. J. and Pandit, R. (1977) reported that creative people displayed better adjustments.

Nair (1976) also found creative individuals to be much more involved in family, school and community relation.

Singh, R.J. (1980) reported creativity to have positive and significant relationship with social, educational and overall adjustment, but not with the emotional adjustment.

In one study social adjustment was found to be higher in the case of high creatives (Sansanwal and Jarial, 1981).

However, on the other hand, McClaund (1962) has reported creatives to be less adjusted and remarked that apathy which characterized the relationship of the eminent scientists with their parents resulted in their withdrawal from human relationship in general and discharging their aggressive impulses through their creative work. Das Gupta, 1977; Ahmad, 1969, and Sharma, 1978, have also found in their studies that poor adjustment in respect of home, health, social and emotional life characterized the high creative group.

Kaur (1979) has also observed high creatives to be confronted with more problems in their socio-psychological areas. Amidst these controversial findings a study on creativity and adjustment was taken up by Sharan, P. The adjustment was measured by administering Mohsin–Shamshad adaptation of Bell adjustment inventory which measures adjustment in respect of home, health, social and emotional life of the individual and also yields scores on his overall adjustment. Higher scores on this inventory indicate poor adjustment and lesser scores a better adjustment. The findings of Sharan, P. revealed that high creative group on verbal and non-verbal test of creativity significantly differed from the low creative group in respect of their adjustment in different areas as well as on overall adjustment. High creative group on verbal and non-verbal creativity both obtained lower mean scores, indicating better adjustment;

as compared to their low counterparts. Hence, it was held that respondents excelling high on creativity enjoyed a healthy home, health and emotional adjustment. as well as overall adjustment. The obtained mean differences were found to be significant at .01 level of confidence. The detailed results are being presented in tabular form as follows:

TABLE 5.1: **The Mean and SD Scores and 't'-value Obtained on Adjustment Inventory (Area-wise and Overall Adjustment) by Two Groups of Subject Categorized as High and Low on Verbal Creativity**

Adjustment	*Groups*	*N*	*Mean*	*Sd*	*df*	*'t' ratio*	*Level of Significance*
Home	High	146	11.39	4.74			
	Low	254	19.80	4.95	398	16.76	P<.01
Health	High	146	8.76	3.90			
	Low	254	14.34	5.53	398	11.75	P<.01
Social	High	146	10.90	3.61			
	Low	254	16.67	5.04	398	13.24	P<.01
Emotional	High	146	13.61	9.03			
	Low	254	20.17	5.04	398	8.07	P<.01
Overall	High	146	44.03	14.88			
	Low	254	71.04	19.06	398	15.67	P<.01

TABLE 5.2: **Non-Verbal Creativity**

Adjustment	*Groups*	*N*	*Mean*	*SD*	*df*	*'t' ratio*	*Level of significance*
Home	High	262	13.94	5.32			
	Low	138	21.94	4.44	398	14.98	P<.01
Health	High			4.38			
	Low	138	16.43	5.39	398	12.73	P<.01
Social	High	262	12.38	4.06			
	Low	138	18.68	3.09	398	13.44	P<.01
Emotional	High	262	15.05	4.73			
	Low	138	22.21	4.97	398	14.09	P<.01
Overall	High	262	51.48	16.76			
	Low	138	79.41	18.42	398	15.26	P<.01

Further, supports to the findings were extended by the results obtained by applying product moment correlation and multiple regression analysis. The coefficients of correlation between scores on creativity and those on adjustment (areawise and overall) were reported to be negative and significant at .01 level. The correlation value ranged between –.542 to –.790 and from –.372 to –.556 for verbal and non-verbal creativity respectively. These values indicated that the higher the adjustment the greater the creativity. However, multiple regression analysis indicated positive contribution of home and overall adjustment to verbal and non-verbal creativity both. This result extended only partial support to the findings based on 't' ratio and simple correlation. The positive contribution of a better home adjustment to creativity had been explained in terms of facilities available at home for growth of creativity and opportunities to channelize the inner resources and abilities of children in a productive and constructive way. A better home adjustment also provides lesser tension and conflicts and generates more confidence. So far health adjustment was concerned the researcher did not obtain its significant contribution towards creativity. The reason may be that healthy and unhealthy persons both can make themselves involved in productive works depending upon the energy and concentration which they have. Unhealthy and diseased persons can also engage themselves in creative writing or other such activities just to minimize the intensity of threat and anxiety caused by their illness. As far as non-significant contribution of emotional adjustment to creativity is concerned, it has already been remarked that even emotionally disturbed people like neurotics or psychotic can produce something novel and original, depending upon their inner conflicts and inner urges. Of course, the analysis of their creative works may reveal something different from that of emotionally stable person. Further, lack of emotional adjustment all the time never means mental disorder. However, it is to be remarked that the greater number of empirical findings are in favour of a positive influence of emotional stability, independence and maturity on the creative behaviour.

In respect of social adjustment it was observed that the greater the social maladjustment the greater the creativity. The researcher had categorically remarked that socially maladjusted persons, because of their feeling of alienation and isolation, may divert their inner potentialities into creative channels. The creative paintings and writings etc. can be a reflection of the individual's discontentment with the existing socio-cultural system. Roe (1951) has also observed creatives to be less conventional and unsocial.

The findings of Mccluand (1962) have been also quoted in support of the present findings. He observed that creative individuals are so much involved in their thoughts that they seem to be withdrawn from the human relationship. Drevdahl (1964) has also found in his study that creative individuals are unusually self-centred and attach less importance to social relationships or criticisms.

These persons show greater interest in creative pursuit than in socially oriented activities, Rahman and Hussain (1973) and Varma (1980), have shown that creative individuals do not care much for social approval. Bhan (1970) observed none of the factors of sociability to be significantly related to creative performance. Das Gupta (1977), while comparing high and low creatives, found the former to exhibit disturbed parental relationship and to be more involved in their own beliefs and attitude. The high creatives, thus, exhibited non-conforming attitude.

Pramesh (1970) has also observed creative individuals to possess lesser sociability and liking for the company of others and exhibiting less co-operation.

Kaur, B (1983) has also reported high creatives to have problems in their socio-psychological areas.

Singh, R. (1975) has, however extended partial support to the above quoted study. He has reported fluency aspect of creativity to be positively and significantly related to family and social adjustment, whereas flexibility had negative significant relationships.

Thus, on the basis of the supporting evidences, Sharan, P. has well argued in favour of her empirical findings in respect of social adjustment and creativity.

While arguing in favour of positive contribution of overall adjustment (based on composite scores) towards verbal and non-verbal creativity, the researcher has reported a number of findings (Drevdahl, 1964; Goyal, 1974; Singh, R. 1975; Gupta, 1976; Nair, 1976; Singh, R.J., 1976; Pandit, R. 1977; Singh, 1980; Sansanwal and Jarial, 1981) which assert that creativity and adjustment are positively and significantly correlated to each other.

Lazarus (1978) has also emphasized creativity to be indirectly associated with better adjustment. Hurlock (1978) has categorically stated that for the most part there is little evidence that children who are creative are maladjusted.

Another significant remark can be made in respect of the study of Sharan, P., which is a pointer to researcher in the area of creativity and adjustment. The researches investigated into the relationship of adjustment (area-wise and overall) only with creativity based on composite scores. She should have found out the relationship of adjustment also with various aspects of creativity like fluency, flexibility, elaboration and originality. This could have better reflected the relationship between these two variables. For example, a person may have positive relationship with social adjustment and fluency but not with flexibility aspect of creativity. The present author, however, admits that for a single researcher it might not have been possible to include elaborate aspects of creativity in all the cases. Hence, further investigations are suggested in order to have a better generalization in respect of adjustment and creativity in a more intensive manner.

Ego Strength and Creativity

Amidst various approaches to the concept of ego a highly systematic approach was made by Freud, who considered it to be the most powerful component of personality.

Ego has been taken to be the executive of personality to maintain balance between the impulses of the Id and the standard of the super ego. The ego is also responsible for an individual's adjustment with the external reality. When ego is threatened it adopts various defence mechanisms to defend itself against the threatening impulses. The functioning of ego was further elaborated by Anna Freud (1964) and then by Hartmann, *et al.* (1958, 1964) who including the adaptive and integrative function of ego granted it an autonomous position. Hartmann extended the role of ego in total personality. He believes that ego defences may not be pathological or negative in character rather, they may be helpful in the formation of personality. These defences may become independent of their origin in combating the instinctual urges and serve the function of adjustment and organization. Ego theorists also argue that certain processes of the ego may not have conflict with the Id, the super ego or with the external world. These processes may be incompatible with one another, so that the individual has to make decision regarding the best way to solve a problem or make adjustment. Others who have argued in favour of the adaptive functioning of the ego are Rapaport, 1960; Gill, 1959 and Klein, 1976. Jung's view (1959) on ego has also been considered to be significant. He described ego as the consicious part of mind which includes perception, memories, thoughts and feelings, which are in the awareness of an individual at a moment. The ego performs the vital function of being selective in perceiving relevant and meaningful stimuli and sensation. Jung also asserts that ego functioning helps in attaining spontaneity, creativity and insight.

Hall and Lindzley (1978) held that the kind of ego that Erikson described may be called the creative ego, which finds creative solutions to new problems by combining inner readiness and outer opportunity whereas thwarted ego reacts with more efforts instead of giving up the problem. In short, it can be remarked that with the rise of ego psychology, the ego was much more considered as a controlling mechanism within the personality.

Fenichel (1945) has summarized the five functions of the ego which include perception, motality, binding tension, judgement and synthesizing. It is the ego which makes an individual aware of himself and his environment. Ego enables a person to adopt appropriate responses to the environmental demands through co-ordination of motor mechanism. Ego controls the instinctual urges from breaking through and also adopts various defences for the purpose of meeting the increasing function. As far as judgement is concerned it involves analysing the various aspects of alternatives. In respect of synthesizing functioning it has been said that ego safeguards an individual from being dragged in different directions.

White, R. (1963) has suggested that ego not only has its own intrinsic energy but there are also intrinsic ego satisfactions which are independent of the Id or the instinctual gratification. These autonomoussa tisfaction of the ego may concern manipulation, exploration and effective competence in performing a task.

Ali (1975) has considered ego strength as an important factor which determines an individual's capacity to perceive a challenging situation in a realistic way and to execute the response in an effective manner.

Hasan, Q. (1976) has stressed that one may not agree with psycho-analytical theory of the structure of personality and yet he may accept the concept of ego strength, if it is defined as the total psychic energy at the disposal of the individual enabling him to enjoy his strivings to master the environment. Such non-psycho-analytic concept as competence motive (White, 1959), Maslow's (1956) self-actualization and psychological health seem to have much in common with ego strength.

In the light of various approaches stated above, in respect of ego one can treat ego as the most powerful structure of an individual's personality which helps in bringing a harmonious and realistic adjustment. While dealing with creativity the conception of creative ego within the personality seems to be distinct as it has concerned with various cognitive processes which may facilitate creative behaviour. Roe (1952) observed independence and self-sufficiency as distinct characterizing feature of the creatives. Munsterberg and Mussen (1953) found creative painters to be more imaginative and curious about things, less conventional and interested in various activities.

Eiduson (1958) also observed artists to have high ego, tolerance and to have unique ways of communicating their feelings and experiences to others. Torrance (1959), studied 240 graduate students for their novel thoughts and found high originals to show high ego beside other factors. Eiduson (1962) while studying the main qualities in scientists on which they differed from non-creative scientists found that the formers were interested in complex intellectual tasks, sensitive towards others and themselves and unconventional and original in approach. Ego strength was found to be involved in their creative work. High ego strength, intelligence and dominance have been also observed to be present in eminent creative scientists (Cattell and Butcher, 1968). The role of high ego strength in creative output has been also emphasized by Joshi, 1974; Calvani, A. *et al.*, 1974 and Jha, 1975. Other important characteristics associated with ego strength were rational opinions, realistic and healthy attitude towards life, openness to experiences. assertiveness, self-confidence and self-actualization.

In the light of such studies with regard to the positive role of ego strength in creativity Sharan, P. (1986) planned and conducted an empirical study under the supervision of the present author to find out whether ego strength positively affect the growth of creative potentials. The study was conducted on a sample of 400 college students in the state of Bihar. The underlying assumption was that the greater the ego strength the greater the creative expression of the individuals, as the ego serves as controlling mechanism and facilitates the analysis and synthesis of various environmental forces. The ego strength was measured by Hindi adapted form of Barron's ego strength scale (Hasan, Q.). The findings of the study are given below.

The correlational findings indicated a significant positive correlation between ego strength and verbal and non-verbal creativity both (r = ·683 and ·468 respectively). High scorers on ego strength scale performed better on test of creativity which indicated that ego strength facilitates in creating something new. Thus, the present study supported the findings of number of investigators, already quoted earlier.

The obtained multiple regression analysis also indicated the independent positive and significant contribution of ego strength towards verbal and non-verbal creativity both. The same findings were obtained by comparing the mean scores on ego strength scale of high and low creative groups in verbal creativity both. The high scorers on creativity obtained higher mean scores on ego strength (26.88 and 23·94 respectively) in comparison to their low counterparts (mean value = 15·41 and 11·37 respectively for verbal and non-verbal creativity).

Thus all the statistical findings in general were supportive of the assumption that ego not only serves a healthy purpose in the formulation of personality but it may also facilitate spontaneity, creativity, insight and deep emotions while performing important functions. While going through the studies on personality characteristics in relation to creativity, the present author remarks that human personality is so complex and multidimensional that simple correlational studies on the relationship between isolated characteristics of personality and creativity are not sufficient to tell something highly dependable. However, he does not categorically discard the study of different variables from a simple correlational angle rather he emphasizes the estimation of joint contribution of these variables toward creativity and also their interactional influence on it. Such studies are needed which not simply determine the influence of single trait or characteristics on creative performance, but also interaction among the traits within themselves and among the traits and cognitive abilities. This will help in analysing the combined effect of personality characteristics on creativity. This requirement was fulfilled to a greater extent, by Sharan, P. (1986) who examined the joint contribution of personality variables towards creativity.

The author, while going through the findings with regard to personality characteristics of creative artists or scientists, has noted that the investigators have simply tried to make observation of these traits in isolation and enlist them. The result has been that the greater the analysis of research findings on personality characteristics, relevant to creativity, the greater the collection of diversified traits or characteristics of creative individuals. These characteristics scatter over a wide range which makes it difficult to have a sound comparable estimate and to generalize some fundamental personality characteristics of creative people.

The efforts are to be made to locate fundamental characteristics of those individuals who are either engaged in various types of creative works or are assessed on verbal and non-verbal tests of creative thinking. In other words, microscopic studies are needed in order to peep into some fundamental personality correlates of creativity. The author, thus, feels that findings based on factor analytical techniques are much needed in order to examine the common clustering of the traits which may restrict unnecessary number of traits.

In the study of Sharan, P. (1986) beside individual contribution of various factors attempt was also made to examine the joint contribution of all the independent variables towards verbal and non-verbal creativity by way of applying regression analysis. The independent variables were socio-economic status, ego strength, home adjustment, health adjustment, social adjustment emotional adjustment, overall adjustment, neuroticism and extraversion and the dependent variable was verbal and non-verbal creativity. The detailed analysis is presented in Table 5.3 and 5.4.

TABLE 5.3 : **Regression Analysis of Verbal Creativity (Dependent Variable) as a Function of Different Independent Variables (SES.,Ego-strength, Adjustment : Home, Health, Social, Emotional and Overall; Extraversion-Introversion and Neuroticism)**

Variables	*Coefficient estimates*	*Standard error*	*'t' value*
SES	0.00009	0.01097	0.00816 N.S.
Ego-strength	0.04091	0.01206	3.39226**
Home adjustment	0.07682	0.02978	–2.57966**
Health adjustment	0.03931	0.03015	1.30409 N.S.
Social adjustment	0.10204	0.04289	2.37930*
Emotional adjustment	–0.03121	0.04067	–0.76744 N.S.
Overall adjustment	–0.5692	0.01647	–3.45585**
Neuroticism	–0.06760	0.01603	–4.21576**
Extraversion	0.03031	0.01823	1.66256 N.S.

Multiple correlation $R^2 = 0.662$.
* = *Significant at* 0.5 *level of confidence.*
** = *Significant at* 0.01 *level of confidence.*
N.S. = *Not significant.*

TABLE 5.4: **Regression Analysis of Non-Verbal Creativity (Dependent Variable) as a Function of Different Independent Variables (SES, Ego-strength, Adjustment : Home, Health, Social, emotional and Overall, Extraversion-Introversion and Neuroticism)**

Variables	*Coefficient estimates*	*Standard error*	*'t' Value*
SES	0.01045	0.00697	1.49971 N.S.
Ego-strength	0.03477	0.00766	4.53987**
Home adjustment	0.04304	0.01891	-2.27605*
Health adjustment	0.01973	0.01914	1.03080 N.S.
Social adjustment	0.07237	0.02724	2.65695**
Emotional adjustment	-0.01058	0.02583	-0.40975 N.S.
Overall adjustment	-0.04342	0.01046	-4.15159**
Neuroticism	-0.03189	0.01018	-3.13114**
Extraversion	0.01438	0.01158	1.24179 N.S.

Multiple correlation R^2=0.6928

* = *Signifieant at* 0.05 *level of confidence.*

** = *Significant at* 0.01 *level of confidence.*

N.S. = *Not significant.*

The analysis of the above tables indicate that the multiple correlation—R^2 is 0·662 and 0.629 for verbal and non-verbal creativity respectively. These findings indicate the extent to which all these variables taken together assert their joint influence on the creativity scores. In the case of verbal creativity the R^2 value suggests that the nine factors taken together explain 66% about verbal creativity which is quite high. In the case of non-verbal creativity they explain about 69% which is also quite high. Hence, the investigator clearly supported the assumption regarding the influence of personality variables, SES and adjustment on creative performance.

The above note on creativity, as related to some personality variables, reflects that it seems difficult to restrict the area of investigation regarding the number of personality factors in relation to creativity. More researches are needed to include various other factors like approval-seeking motive, religiosity, dominance, achievent motivation, conservation, etc., in order to examine their contribution toward creativity.

Further, the author feels that studies like that of Sharan, P. (1986) should be conducted to examine the joint contribution of a number of related personality variables beside their independent contribution to creativity. Such findings would present a comprehensive picture of such variables, as they contribute jointly towards creative behaviour in interaction with one another.

APPENDIX

A BATTERY OF CREATIVITY TESTS

(*Verbal and Non-Verbal*)
in Hindi

by

Dr. Baqer Mehdi (*Professor of Education N.C.E.R.T., New Delhi*)

Baqer Mehdi's (1973) test of creative thinking is an adapted form of Torrance test of creative thinking. The total battery is composed of verbal and non-verbal tests both.

The battery is meant to identify creative talent at all stages of education, except pre-primary and primary. The battery was standardized on a sample of urban and rural students from Punjab and U.P. On the basis of the item analysis it has been reported that both the verbal and non-verbal tests are highly internally consistent, and seem to measure a unified dimension in the intellectual domain which can justifiably be designated as creativity.

The verbal test consists of four sub-tests : consequences test, unusual test, similarity test, and product improvement test.

(1) *Consequences Test* : The consequences test consists of three hypothetical situations : (a) What would happen if man could fly like bird ? (b) What would happen if the schools had wheels ? (c) What would happen if man does not have any need for food ?

The subjects are instructed to think of as many consequences of the given situations in the test as he can, and write them under each situation in the space provided to them. The situations are hypothetical and hence minimize the effect of experience and also provide the subject with an unlimited opportunity to give responses. This test provides an opportunity for the subject's free play of imagination and his originality. Various examples are given on the test booklet to make the subjects acquainted with the nature of the test. Four minutes are given for three problems each.

(2) *Unusual Uses Test* : Unusual uses test presents names of three common subjects, such as a piece of stone, a wooden stick, and water—and the testee is asked to write as many novel, interesting and unusual uses of these objects in the test booklet given to him. The testee is further asked to think in relation to the problem. The test is a measure of subject's ability to retrieve items of information from his/her personal information or abilities to think on the problem in a novel and original way. Evidently, it attempts to measure whether the subject can shift his frames of reference to use the environment

in an original manner. Five minutes are given for each of the three kinds of activities.

(3) *New Relationships test* : New Relationships test consists of three pairs of words which are apparently different : tree and house, chair and ladder, and air and water. This test is given to subject and he is required to think and report all possible relationships between the two objects of each pair of words in the space provided. The test provides an opportunity for free play of imagination and originality of the testees. The time provided for the completion of each pair of words is five minutes.

(4) *Product Improvement Test* : In this test the subject is asked to think of a simple wooden toy of a horse and to suggest addition of new things to it, so that the wooden imaginary toy may look more interesting for the children to play. The time for the completion of wooden horse is six minutes only.

Thus, the time required for the total test is 48 minutes in addition to the time necessary for giving instructions, passing out test booklets to the subjects and collecting them back.

Each item of the test booklet is scored for fluency, flexibility and originality. The definitions of these terms are given for the purpose of clarifying the concept of the terms used.

Verbal Fluency

Fluency is represented by the number of relevant and unrepeated ideas which the testee produces. Relevancy is determined or judged on the basis of the appropriateness of the response when considered in relation to the test problem. An unrepeated idea is one which has been expressed only once under a given problem.

Verbal Flexibility

This represents the ability of a person to produce a variety of ideas, to shift from one approach to another or use various strategies. All ideas which come under one or single category of approach or thought trend are treated as one for purpose of flexibility scoring. Thus, if six ideas are produced and all belong to one category of thought trend, then the score for the flexibility will be one, but if all the six ideas belong to six different approaches or thought trend then the flexibility score will be six. There could be intermediate scores for flexibility depending on the number of categories of thought trends to which the responses belong.

Verbal Originality

Originality is represented by uncommonness of a given response. Responses given by less than 5% of the subjects are treated as original. These scores represent the subject's ability to produce ideas that are away from the obvious and established thought. The person who achieves a high score on verbal originality usually has the availability of a great deal of intellectual energy and is perceived as non-conforming. He is able to make big mental leaps or 'cut corners' in obtaining solutions of the problems. However, this does not mean that the person is erratic or impulsive. In fact, the original responses require the ability to delay immediate gratification or reduction of tension in order to get away from the obvious, easy, but low quality response.

Thus, Verbal Test of Creative Thinking is scored in three directions or areas: fluency, flexibility and originality.

BAQER MEHDI's NON-VERBAL TEST OF CREATIVITY THINKING

Non-verbal test of creative thinking is a part of the total battery of creativity which consists of verbal test also. The non-verbal test of creative thinking is intended to measure the individual's ability to deal with figural content in a creative fashion. Three types of activity are used for this purpose, viz. (a) picture construction, (b) picture completion and (c) triangles and ellipses. The total time required for administering the test is 35 minutes, in addition to the time necessary for giving instructions, passing out booklets and collecting them back.

A brief description of the non-verbal test of creative thinking is as follows:

(1) *Picture Construction Activity*

In picture construction activity, the testee is required to construct two simple geometrical figures, a semi circle and a rhomb, and to construct an elaborate picture using each figure as an integral part. The subject may turn the page to use the figure in any way he likes for making the picture. Emphasis is put on originality and elaboration. Originality is emphasized by way of instructing the subject that he should try to make as novel a picture as possible such that no one else will be able to produce. Elaboration is emphasized by the instruction that the subject may add as many details as he thinks necessary in order to make the picture tell as complete and as interesting a story as possible. Ten minutes are allowed for the two tasks.

The pictures are scored for elaboration and originality. The subject is also required to give an interesting and unusual title to each picture. The titles may also be scored for verbal elaboration and originality and the scores be added to the verbal creativity score obtained on the verbal creativity test. However, the scoring of titles is optional.

(2) *Incomplete Figures Activity*

This activity consists of 10 line drawings which could be made into meaningful pictures of different objects. The subject is asked to make a picture which no one else in the group will be able to think of. He is also asked to give an interesting and suitable title to each picture he makes. 15 minutes are given for the 10 items. Each item is scored for elaboration and originality. Titles may also be scored for verbal elaboration and originality and the scores be added to the verbal creativity score, obtained on the verbal creativity test. However, the scoring of titles is optional.

(3) *Triangles and Ellipses Activity*

In this activity the subject is provided with 7 triangles and 7 ellipses and he is required to construct different meaningful pictures based on two given stimuli. The subject is here encouraged to make multiple association to single stimulus, hence, the responses might be scored for flexibility besides elaboration and originality, but as this is the only activity in which flexibility scoring is possible, it is recommended that here too the test user should confine himself to the scoring of elaboration and originality alone. A total time of 10 minutes is given for this activity.

The subject is also required to give an interesting and suitable title to each picture which may also be scored for verbal elaboration and originality and the scores be added to the verbal creativity score, obtained on the verbal creativity test. The scoring of the titles, however, is optional.

The three activities, taken together, provide an opportunity to the subject to use his imagination with different types of figural tasks and come out with some novel ideas.

Each item is to be scored for elaboration and originality. Only the items in Activity III may be scored for flexibility also. Flexibility scoring, however, is optional. The definitions of these terms are given below:

Elaboration

Elaboration is represented by a person's ability to add pertinent details (more ideas) to the minimum and primary response to the stimulus figure. The minimum and the primary response to the stimulus figure is that response which gives essential meaning to the picture. The response title often tells what exactly the testee is trying to make. However, responses which can be reasonably interpreted and identified should be scored. In some cases, the test booklets will have to be turned around in order to know exactly what the testee has drawn. Sometimes the response represents some abstract idea instead of a thing and so it has got to be scored.

Originality

Originality is represented by uncommonness of a given response. Responses given only by less than 5 per cent of the group are considered and are given differential weights. The weights have to be determined on the basis of the following scheme: If a response has been given by 1 per cent to .99 per cent of the testees, the response will get an originality weight of 5; if a response has been given by 1 per cent to 1.99 per cent of the testees, then the response will get an originality score of 4; if a response has been given by 2 per cent to 2.99 per cent of the testees, then the response will get an originality score of 3, if a response has been given by 3 per cent to 3.99 per cent of the testees, then the response will get an originality weight of 2; if the response has been given by 4 per cent to 4.99 per cent of the testees, then the response will get an originality weight of 1. Responses given by 5 per cent or more of the testees will get an originality weight of zero.

Flexibility

Flexibility is represented by a person's ability to produce ideas which differ in approach for thought trend. All ideas which differ in approach or thought trend are treated as one for purposes of flexibility scoring. Thus, if five ideas are produced and all belong to only one category of approach or thought trend, the score for flexibility will be one, but if all the five ideas are based on five different approaches or thought trends, then the flexibility score will be 5.There could be intermediate scores for flexibility, depending on the number of categories of thought trends to which the responses belong.

In the non-verbal test, only activity III, viz. Triangles and Ellipses may be scored for flexibility as the testee is asked to make different picture, from the same given stimulus. But as has been noted above, since this is the only activity in which flexibility scoring is possible and the scores have to be based on two items alone, not much confidence can be placed on the reliability of these scores.

The item-sum correlations for the verbal test (urban sample) range from .555 to .768, while for the non-verbal test they range from .200 to .652. In the case of the rural sample the item-sum correlations for the verbal test range from .412 to .692 and for the non-verbal test they range from .184 to .530. The correlations of items with the total activity scores are much higher indicating that the items are internally consistent. In the urban sample the correlations of items with their total activity scores for the verbal test range from .766 to .882 and for the non-verbal test they range from .533 to .936, barring only two which are correlated to the extent of .176 and .377, both being significant at .01 level. In the case of rural sample, the correlations of items with their total activity scores for the verbal test range from .668 to .798 and for the non-verbal test they range from .308 to .703.

The correlations of total activity scores with the grand total are also substantially high. In the urban sample, they range from .761 to .862 for the verbal test and from .634 to .941 for the non-verbal test. In the rural sample these correlations range from .541 to .741 for the verbal test and .312 to .580 for the non-verbal test. The inter-correlations among the four activities of the verbal test (urban sample) range from .457 to .637 and among the three activities of the non-verbal test, they range from .303 to .477. In the rural sample these correlations range from .163 to .321 among the four verbal activities of the verbal test and from .071 to .143 for the three activities of the non-verbal test. The relatively low intercorrelations among the test activities and their high correlations with the grand totals indicate that while among themselves they are not entirely measuring the same thing, each one is contributing significantly to the total creativity score.

The factor scores, i.e. scores for fluency, flexibility, and originality (verbal), and elaboration and originality (non-verbal) also give substantially high correlations with the total creativity scores. In the urban sample the factor-sum correlations for the verbal test range from .889 to .966 and for the non-verbal test thay range from .786 to .875. In the rural sample, these correlations range from .751 to .823 for the verbal test and from .539 to .604 for the non-verbal test.

Correlation with Intelligence

Another important finding which enables us to place high reliance on the tests is their significant but considerably low correlations with verbal and non-verbal tests of intelligence. In the rural sample where Raven's Progressive Matrices was used, the correlations with verbal and non-verbal creativity tests were found to be .194 and .181 respectively. In the urban sample where Mohsin's verbal group test of intelligence was used the correlations with verbal and non-verbal creativity tests came out to be .176 and .139 respectively.

Correlations between the Verbal and non-Verbal Tests of Creativity

The correlations between the verbal and non-verbal tests of creativity, based on the total creativity scores, were found to be .456 and .356 for the urban and rural samples respectively, indicating that while two tests are measuring the same construct, namely, creativity, they are giving somewhat different information about it. It is recommended that both the tests should be used to have more complete information about the creativity of an individual. Validity studies will indicate which type of creativity score is more specifically related to creativity performance in a particular field.

Reliability and Validity of the Tests

Test-retest reliabilities of both the tests are quite high. For the total creativity score the reliabilities for verbal and non-verbal tests (N=31 and 50) are .959 and .946 respectively. For factor scores the reliabilities range from .896 to .945 for the verbal test, and from .823 to .947 for the non-verbal test.

Inter-scores reliabilities for the factor scores in one study were found to range from .65 to .98.

Validities with teacher ratings ranged from .29 to .40 for fluency, .31 to .34 for flexibility and from .26 to .39 for originality. In another validation study, where teacher ratings on ten personality traits relevant to creative thinking were used, the correlations with the total rating came out to be .222 for the verbal test and .385 for the non-verbal test.

Norms have been worked out for classes VII and VIII.

With all the data now available, the battery can profitably be used by research workers as well as school authorities who would be interested in identifying creative talent from class VII onwards.

BIBLIOGRAPHY

Agarwal, Y.P. and L.K. Verma (1977). 'External Control of High Creative and Low Creative High School Students at Different Levels of Socio-economic Status'. *Journal of Creative Behaviour*, 2, (2) 1950.

Ahmad, N. (1969). 'A Study of the Personality Correlates of Creative Girls at the Middle School Age.' Unpublished M.A. (Psychology) dissertation, Aligarh Muslim University, Aligarh, 1969.

Ahmad, S. (1980). 'Effect of Socio-culture Disadvantage on Creative Thinking'. *Journal of Psychological Researches*, 24, (2), 96-106.

Aldous, J. (1973). 'Family Background Factors and Originality in Children'. *Gifted Child* Quarterly, 17, 183-192.

Aldous, Joan, (1975). 'The Search for Alternative: Parental Behaviours and Children's Original Problem Solutions'. *Journal of Marriage and Family*, 37(4), 711-722.

Ali, S.N. and Ahmad S. (1975). 'Perceptual Vigilance in High and Low Ego-Strength Individuals'. Part-III of the *Proceedings of the 62nd Session of Indian Science Congress Association.*

Aliotti, N.C. (1969). 'The Effects of Warm-up Activities on the First Grade Children'. Doctoral Dissertation. University of Georgia. Dissertation Abstracts, 30, 5275-A.

Anderson, J.E. (1960). 'The Nature of Abilities', in E.P. Torrance (Ed.) *Education and Talent.* Minnesota, University of Minnesota Press.

Ausubel, D.P. (1958). *Theory and problems of Child Development.* N.Y. Grune and Stratton.

Awasthy, M. (1979). 'A Study of Creativity, Intelligence, Scholastic Achievement and the Factors of Socio-Economic Status'. Unpublished M.Ed. Dissertation, Indore University.

Barchillon, J. (1961). 'Creativity and Inhibition in Child Prodigies Personality Dimension of Creativity, Lincoln Institute of Psychotherapy', N.Y. In E.P. Torrance's *Rewarding Creative Talent: Experiments in Class Room Creativity.* Englewood Cliff, N.J. Prentice Hall.

Barker Lunn, J.C. (1970). 'Streaming in the Primary School'. *Research Report.* London, National Foundation for Educational Research.

Barron, F. (1961). *Psychological Vitality and Creative freedom.* New York, Wiley.

Barron, F. (1962). 'The Creative Writer'. *California Man,* 72 (5) 11-14, 38-39.

Barron, F. (1963). 'Creativity and Psychological Health'. Princeton, N. J. Van Nostrand.

Barron, F. (1969). 'The Creative Person and the Creative Process'. N. Y. Holt.

Barron, F. (1975). The disposition toward originality. Referred in Calvin

W. Taylor and Frank Barron's *Scientific Creativity*: New York, Robert E. Krieger Publishing Co., Huntington.

Bhan, Rajnath (1970). 'Social Factors in Creative Potentiality'. *Manas*, 17(1), 21-27.

Bhardwaj, R.L. and R.P. Gupta (1980). 'Fluency, Intelligence and Socio-economical Status as Correlates of the Interest in Scientific Pursuits'. *Asian Journal of Psychology and Education*, 6(3) 23-30.

Bhargava, M. (1979). 'Personal Variables and Second Order Personality Correlates of Creativity. *Indian Psychological Review*, 17, 3-4, 63-67.

Bhattacharya, P.S. (1956). Referred in *Creativity in Education*, Agra (India) National Psychological Corporation, 11, 1982.

Binet, Alfred, (1909). *Les Idees Modernes Sur Les Enfants*, Paris, E. Flamarion.

Bishop, D. W. and Charles, A. Chase (1971). 'Paternal Conceptional System, Home Play, Environment and Potential Creativity in Children. *Journal of Experimental Child Psychology*. 12(3), 318-338.

Bless, W., J. Halvsa, and Va Thormanno (1981). 'Status of Creative Personality in the Group.' *Psychological Abstract*, No. 3238 Vol. 65, No. 2.

Borad, J., J.C. Grossman and Russel Eiseman, (1971). 'Extraversion, Anxiety Creativity and Grade'. *Perceptual and Motor Bills*, 33 (3.2), 1106.

Bourne, Jr. L.E. and R. Ekstrand Bruce (1973). *Psychology: It's Principles and meaning*. The Dryden Press Hinsdale, Illinois.

Bowers, Kenneth, S. (1971). 'Sex and Susceptibility as Moderator Variables in the Relationship of Creativity and Hypnotic Suggestibiltiy'. *Jounal of Abnormal Psychology*, 78(1), 93-100.

Brunelle, E.A. (1970). 'Creative Intelligence and Freshmen English Problem'. *Journal of Genetic Psychology*, 1971, 118, 3-12.

Bruner, J.S. (1961). *The Process of Education*. Cambridge, Mass: Harvard University Press. C.f. Butcher, H.J. (1970).

Bruner, J.S. (1964). 'The Course of Cognitive Growth'. *American Psychologist*, 19, 1-15.

Burt and Verma (1950). 'Dynamics of Creativity'. National Psychological Corporation, Agra, India. C.F. Sharma, K.N. (1979).

Burt, C. (1962). Critical Notice of 'Creativity and Intelligence' by Getzels and Jackson. *Brit. J. educ. Psychol*, 32, 292-298.

Butcher, H. J. (1970). *Human Intelligence: Its Nature and Assessment*. Great Britain, Bulter and Tanner.

Cacha, F.B. (1971). 'A Study of the Relation of Creative Thinking Abilities to Personality Factors and Peer Nomination of Fifth Grade Children'. *Dissertation Abstracts International*, 1971, 32, 1329-A.

Calvani, A. and M.P. Cesaretti, (1974). Creativity and Social Attitudes, *Bolletio di Psychologia Applicata*, 1974 (Aug.-Dec.), No. 124-126, 107-128.

Cameron, Marion B. (1967). 'An Investigation of Cognitive Differences in

First Year Arts and Science Students'. M. Ed. Thesis. University of Aberdeen. Cf. Butcher, H. J. (1970).

Cattell, R.B. and Drevdahl J.E. (1955). A Comparison of the Personality Profile (16. P. F.) of Eminent Researchers with that of Eminent Teachers and Administrators and of the General Population. *Brit. J. Psychol.* 44, 248-261. Cf. Butcher, H. J. (1970).

Cattell, R. B. (1958). *Personality and Motivation Structure and Measurement.* New York, World Book Co.

Cattell, R.B. (1963). 'The Interaction of Hereditary and Environmental Influences', *Brit. J. statist. Psychol,* 16, 191-210.

Cattell, R.B. and Butcher, H.J. (1968). 'The Prediction of Achievement and Creativity'. *Indianapolish, Indiana Bobbs Merrill.* Cf. Butcher H. J. (1970).

Chadha, N. K. and Sen, A. K. (1981). 'Creativity as a Function of Intelligence, Socio-economic Status and Sex among 12th Grade School Students'. *Journal of Education and Psychology,* 39, (1) 52-56.

Chauhan, N.S. (1977) 'Second Stratum Personality Factors, Sex, and Age Adolescence as Correlates of Originality. *Indian Psychological Review,* 14, (1) 15-21.

Choudhary, N.C. (1977). *Munda Social Structure.* Ferma K L.M. Private Limited.

Clark, *et al.* (1965). 'Convergent Thinking Abilities of Talented Adolescent'. *Journal of Educational Psychology,* 56(2), 157-163.

Clarke, C. M., Veldman D. J. and Thorpe J. S. (1965). 'Convergent and Divergent Thinking Abilities of Talented Adolescents, *J. Educ. Psychol,* 56, 157-163.

Cline, V. B., Richards J.M. and ABE C. (1962). 'The Validity of a Battery of Creativity Tests in a High School Sample' *Edu. Psychol. Measmt.,* 22, 781-784.

Cline, V.B., Richards J. M. and Needham W.E. (1963). 'Creativity Tests and Achievements in High School Science. *J. appl. Psychol.,* 47, 184-189.

Coopar, Jeol B. and Richmond Bert O (1975). 'Intelligence, Creativity and Performance Abilities of EMR Pupils. *Psychology in Schools,* 12(3), 304-309.

Cropley, A.J. (1966). 'Creativity and Intelligence'. *Brit. J. educ. Psychol.* 36 259-266.

Cropley A.J. (1967). *Creativity Education Today.* London, Longmans, Green and Co.

Cross, P., Cattell R.B. and Butcher H.J. (1967). The Personality Pattern of Creative Artists'. *Brit. J educ. Psychol,* 37, 292-299.

Cross, S. J. (1966). 'The Relation of Parental Training Condition to Conceptual Level in Adolescent Boys. *Journal of Personality,* 34(3).

Crutchfield, R. S. (1962). 'Conformity and Creative Thinking', referred in

H.E. Gruber, G. Terrell and M. Wertheimer's *Contemporary Approaches to Creative Thinking*. N.Y., Athertton Press.

Csondorne Schuller, Gabriella, (1978). 'Hungarian Academy of Science, Psychological Inst. Budapest: The Forming Creativity Factors and their Comparison with the VQ in Five to Six Year Old Children'. (Hung) *Magyar Pszichological Szemle*, 1978, Vol. 35(2), 120-126. Cf. *Psychological Abstract*, No. 5086, March, 1981.

Czerw Jaslewicz, Maria (1979) 'Intelligence and Creative Ability as Specific Dimensions of Intellectual Functioning'. (Polh) *Psychologia Wychowawcza*, 1979 May-June Vol. 22(3), 317-328. Cf. *Psychological Abstract*, No. 13502, Vol. 65, No. 6, June, 1981.

Dasgupta, S. (1977). *Creativity in Education*, Agra, National Psychological Corporation.

Datta, L. (1964). 'A Note on the Remote Associates Test, U.S. culture, and creativity', *J. appl. Psychol.*, 48, 184.

Dauw, D.C. (1966). 'Life Experience, Vocational Needs, and Choices of Original Thinkers and Good Elaborators'. *Dissertation Abstracts* 26, 9, 5223.

Day, H. (1968). 'A Curious Approach to Creativity'. *Canadian Psychologist*, 9(4), 485-497.

Day, H. I. and R. Langevin (1969). 'Curiosity and Intelligence: Two Necessary Conditions for High Level of Creativity'. *Journal of Special Education*, 3(3), 263-268.

De. B. (1984). 'Cognitive Style and Cognitive Ability of Tribal and Non-tribal High School Pupils: A Comparative Study'. Unpublished NCE-RT Project.

Dellas, Marie (1978). 'Creative Personality and Identity'. *Psychological Report*, (Dec.) 43, 3(pt. 2) 1103-1110.

De Mille, R., and P.R. Merrifield (1962). Review of *Creativity and Intelligence* by Getzels and Jackson. *Educ. Ptychol. Measmt.*, 22, 803-808. Cf. Butcher, H. J. (1970).

Dewey, John (1910). *How we think*. Bostan D.C. Health and Co.

Dhir, S. (1973). 'Performance of High School Students on Verbal and Figural Tests of Creative Thinking'. Master's Dissertation, Punjabi University.

Donn Byrne, *et al.* (1981). *An Introduction to Personality*. Parentice Hall.

Drevdahl, J.E. (1956). 'Factors of Importance for Creativity'. *Journal of Clinical Psychology*, 21-26.

Drevdahl, J.E. & Cattell R.B. (1958). 'Personality and Creativity in Artists and Writers'. *Journal of Clinical Psychology*, 14, 107-111.

Drevdahl, J.E. (1964). 'Some Development and Environmental Factors in Creativity', in C.W. Taylor's (Ed.) *Widening Horizons in Creativity*. N.Y. Willey.

Dunnette, M.D. (1964). 'Critics of Psychological Tests: Basic Assumptions:

How Good?' *Psychol. in lhe Schools,* I, 63-69. Cf. Butcher, H. J. (1970).

Dutt, *et al.* (1973) Cf A.V. Madnawat (1986). 'A Study of Creativity in Relation to Intelligence and Manifest Anxiety of Higher Secondary School Boys. Unpublished Ph.D. thesis, University of Rajasthan, Jaipur.

Earl, S. C. (1973). 'A Cross-cultural Study of Creative Thinking and Environmental Factors'. *British Journal of Psychology,* 38, 288-303.

Edwards, Meredith Payne and Leona, E. Tayler (1965). 'Intelligence, Creativity and Achievement in Non-selective Public Junior High School'. *Journal of Educational Psychology,* 56(2), 96-99.

Eiduson, B. T. (1958). 'Artist and Non-Artist: A Comparative Study'. *Journal of Personality,* 26, 13-27.

Eiduson, B. T. (1962). *Scientists; Their Psychological World.* N. Y. Basic Books,

Eisenman, R. and D. J. Foxman (1970). 'Creativity: Reported Family Patterns and Scoring Methodology', *Psychological Reports* 26(1), 267-271.

Elliot, T.D. and F.E. Merrill (1947). *Social Disorganization.* Prentice Hall, 165, 9.

English H.B. and A.C. English (1958). *A Comprehensive Dictionary of Psychological and Psycho-analytical Terms.* N.Y., David Mokay.

Eysenck, H. J. (1947), *Dimension of Personality.* London, Routledge & Kegan Paul.

Eysenck, H. J. (1967). 'Intelligence Assessment: A Theoretical and Experimental Approach'. *British Journal of Educativnal Psychology,* 37, 81-93.

Feld, S.C. (1967). Longitudinal Study of Origins of Achievement Strivings. *Journal of Personality and Social Psychology,* 7(4) 408-414.

Fenichel, O. (1945). *The Psychoanalytic Theory of Neurosis,* N. Y., Norton & Co. Inc.

Flescher, I. (1963). 'Anxiety and Achievement of Intellectually Gifted and Creatively Gifted Children', *J. Psychol.,* 56, 251-268.

Fletcher, K.R. (1968). Congruence of self and Ideal-self in original and Non-original High School seniors. *Dissertation Abstracts,* 28, 11, 4907-A. Cf. Butcher, H. J. (1970).

Forman, Susan, G. (1979). 'Effect of Socio-economic Status on Creativity in Elementary School Children'. *Creative Child and Adult Quarterly,* Vol. 4(2), 8792.

Freud, Anna. (1964). *The Ego and the Mechanism of Defense.* New York, International University Press.

Freeman, Frank, S. (1965). *Theory and Practice of Psychological Testing* (Indian Edn.) Calcutta, Oxford & I B H Publication.

Fromm, Erich (1959). The Creative Attitude. Referred in H.H. Anderson, *Creativity and Its Cultivation.* M.Y. Harper and Row, 44-54.

Fuqua, (1967). Research described in *Times Educ. Supplt.* No. 2715, 1959 (Issue of 2nd June). Cf. Butcher, H. J. (1970).

Gagneja, S.C. (1972). 'A Study of Creativity in Ninth Class Students in Relation to Sex, Residential Background, Academic Achievement, and Parental Occupation'. Master's Dissertation, Punjabi University.

Gakhar, Sudesh & J.N. Joshi (1980). 'Creativity Within the Framework of Personological Centre'. *Psychological Studies*, 26, (1) 48-57.

Getzels, J.W. and P.W. Jackson (1962). *Creativity and Intelligence.* N. Y., John Wiley and Sons.

Ghiselin, B. (1952). *The Creative Process.* N.Y., Mentor Books, New American Library.

Gill, M.M. (1959). 'The Present State of Psycho Analytic Theory'. *Journal of abnormal and social psychology*, 58, 1-8.

Ginsburg, Gerald, P. and Robert G. Whittemore (1968). 'Creativity and Verbal Ability: A Direct Examination of their Relationship. *British Journal of Educational Psychology*, 38(2), 133-139.

Glover J.A. (1973). 'The Effects of Three Reinforcement Contingencies on Creative Responding. University of Tennessee. *Dissertation Abstracts*, 34, 4866-a.

Goldman, R.J. & D.F. Clarke (1967). 'The Minnesota Tests of Creative Thinking: A Note on Scorer Reliability in follow up Studies with English Primary School children', *Brit. J; Edu. Psychol,*, 37, 115-116.

Goldner, B.B. (1962). *The strategy of creative thinking.* Englewood Cliffs, N. J., Prentice Hall.

Goyal, R.P. (1974), 'A Study of Some Personality Correlates of Creativity in Secondary School Teachers under Training'. Ph.D. Thesis, Educ Punjab Univ.

Guilford, J.P. (1950). 'Creativity'. *Amer. Psychologist*, 14, 469-479.

Guilford, J.P. (1956). The Structure of Intellect, *Psychol. Bull.*, 53, 267-293.

Guilford, J.P. and P. R. Christensen (1956). 'Factor Analytic Study of Verbal Fluency'. *Rep. Psychol. Lab.* 17, Los Angles University Southern California.

Guilford, J.P. (1957). 'A Revised Structure of Intellect'. *Report of Psychological Lab.* Los Angeles University of Southern California, 69-95.

Guilford, J.P. (1959). *Personality.* New York, McGraw Hill.

Guilford, J.P. (1959). 'Three Faces of intellect'. *Amer. Psychologist*, 14, 469-479. Reprinted in Anderson and Ausubel (1965).

Guilford, J.P. (1963). 'Potentiality for Creativity and its Measurement', in *Proceedings of the* 1962 *invitational conference on testing Problems.* Princeton N.G. ETS. Cf. Butcher, H. J. (1970).

Guilford, J.P. (1964). 'Progress in Discovery of Intellectual Factors'. In C.W. Taylor's (Ed.) *Widening Horizons of Creativity.* N.Y., Wiley.

Guilford, J.P. (1968). *Intelligence, Creativity and their educational implications.* Son Diego, Calif. R.R. Knapp.

Gulati, S. (1979). 'Creativity as a Function of Intelligence, Artistic Aptitude and Neuroticism'. *Educational trends.* 14, 35-44.

Gupta, K., B. Nisha and R.P. Singh (1976). 'Creative Thinking Abilities and Creative personality—A Study of Relationship of Verbal Creative Thinking Abilities and Creative Personailty'. *Psycho-lingua*, 6 No. (1) 15-18.

Gupta, S. (1986). 'Creativity'. *International Conference on Creativity.*

Haber, R.N. and A.H. Fried (1975). *An introduction to Psychology.* New York, Holts. Rinehart.

Haddon, F.A. and H. Lytton (1968). 'Teaching Approach and the Development of Divergent Thinking Abilities in Primary Schools', *British Journal of Educational Psychology*, 38, 171-180.

Hall, Calvin, S. and Lindzey Gardner (1978). *The Theory of Personality* (3rd edn.), John Willey & sons Inc.

Hammer, E.F. (1961). *Creativity* N.Y., Random House.

Harlow, S.D. (1967). 'Development of the Originality Indicator of Creative Ability'. *Dissertation Abstracts*, 28, 6, 2094-A.

Harvey, O.J., D.E. Hunt and H.M. Schroder (1961). *Conceptual Systems and Personality Organization.* New York, Wiley.

Hartmann, H. *et al.*, (1958). *Ego Psychology and the Problem of Adaptation.* New York, International Universities Press.

Hartmann, H. (1964). *Essays on ego psychology: Selected problems in Psychoanalytic theory* New York, International Universities Press.

Hasan Qamar and Shamsur R. Khan 'Creativity, Intelligence and temperament: A Study of Inter-relationship'. *Psychologia*, 19(4), 193-199.

Heist, P. (1967). 'College Transients', in P. Heist's (Ed.) *Education for Creativity in the American College*, University of California, Centre for Research and Development in Higher Education.

Hudson, L. (1965). 'Intelligence: Convergent and Divergent', *Penguin Science Survey.*

Hurlock, E.B. (1956). *Child Development*, Third Edn., N.Y., McGraw Hill.

Hurlock, E. B. (1978). *Child Development.* Sixth Edition, McGraw Hill Kogakusha Ltd.

Hurlock, E.B. (1978). *Developmental Psychology.* Fourth Edn. (TMH Edition) N.Y. McGraw Hill, 88-195.

Hussain, M. Ghalib and Q. Hussain (1975). 'Cultural Roles, Sex Difference and Creativity' *Educatianal Trends*, 10, 2, 141-145.

Hussain, S. (1985a). *Adjustment and Its Measurement.* New Delhi, S. Chand and Company Ltd.

Hussain, S. (1985b). 'A Cross-cultural Study of Creativity'. Paper accepted for presentation at International Congress of Cross cultural Psychology held at Stanbul, Turkey.

Iwata, Osamu. (1960). 'Some Relationship of Creativity with Intelligence and Personality Variables'. *Psychologia*, 11(3-4), 211-220.

Jacobsen, T.L. and J.J. Asher (1963). 'Validity of the Concept Constancy Measure of Creative Problem Solving'. *Journal of General Psychology*, 68(1), 9-19.

Jacobs, John, F and Myron A Cunningham (1969). 'Creativity and intelligence: Their Relation to Peer Acceptance', *Journal of Special Education,* 3(3), 269-274.

Janssen, C. (1968). 'Comparative Creativity Scores of Lower Socio-economic Drop-Outs and Non-Drop-Outs'. *Psychology in School,* 5, 183-184.

Jarial, Gurpal Singh & A. K. Sharma (1980). 'Creativity and Its Components as Affected by Intelligence, Personality and their Interaction'. *Asian Journal of Psychology and Education,* 6 (21) 26-32.

Jarial, Gurpal Singh (1981). 'Creativity and Family Size'. *Journal of Education and Psychology.*

Jersild, Arthur, T. Charles, W. Telford and James, M. Sawrey (1978). *Child Psychology,* Seventh Edn. New Delhi, Prentice-Hall.

Jha, S.K. (1975). 'An Analysis of Certain Dimensions of Creativity'. *Doctoral Thesis Edn.,* MSU, Baroda.

Johnson, R.A. (1973). 'Differential Effects of Immediate Verses Delayed Reward Instructions on the Creative Thinking of Economic Levels of Elementary School Children'. University of Georgia. *Dissertation Abstract,* 34, 4873-1.

Johnson, D.M. and L. Max (1974). 'Creative Aptitudes in a High Intelligence Population'. *Journal of General Psychology,* 91 (1), 93-104.

Joshi, R.J. (1974). A Study of Creativity and Some Personality Traits of the Intellectually Gifted High School Students *Doctoral Thesis Educ,* MSU.

Jung, C. G. (1959). *The Shadow.* Collected Works, 9, (II) Princeton, Princeton University Press.

Kaplan, Louis (1965). *Foundation of Human Behaviour.* New York, Harper and Row.

Karlins, M. and H.M. Schroder (1967). Discovery Learning Creativity and Inductive Teaching Program'. *Psychological Reports,* 20, 3(1), 867-876.

Kaur, Prakash (1979). 'The Definitions of Creativity and Original Research: Children in the Class Room (Malagsia') *Journal Pondidikan,* U.K.M. No. 4, 18-24.

Kaur, B. (1983). 'A Factor Study of Self Concept, Creativity and Problem Solving among Higher Secondary Students of Indore City'. Unpublished M. Ed. Dissertation, Indore University, Indore.

Kelley, G.R. (1965). 'Creativity, School Attitude and Intelligence Relationships in Grades Four, Six and Eight'. *Dissertation Abstract* 25, 11, 6390. Cf. Sharma, K.N. (1979).

Khatena, Joe (1971). 'Teaching Disadvantaged Pre-School Children to Think Creativity with Pictures'. *Journal of Educational Psychology,* 62, 384-386.

Klin, G.S. (1976). *Perception, motives and personality,* New York, Knopp.

Kogan, Nathan and F.T. Morgan (1969). 'Task and Motivational Influences on the Assessment of Creative and Intellective Ability in Children'. *Genetic Psychology Monograph*, 80, 91-127.

Kogan, Nathan, (1974). 'Creativity and Sex Difference'. *Journal of Creative Behaviour*, 8(1), 1-4.

Kovacova, Eva (1979). Reflection of Some of the Characteristic of the Family and School Environment in Creative Performance (Research Institute of Child Psychology and Psycholopathology), *Psychological Abstract* No. 3072 Vol. 65, No. 2, Feb. 1981.

Kumar A. (1981). 'Personality Identification of High and Low Creative at Age 13 or Older. *Journal of Creative Behaviour*, 15(1) 73.

Lal Ramji (1986). 'A Projective Study of Personality dynamics of Creative Adolescents. *Proceedings. 74th session of Ind. Scic. Congress.*

Lazarus, R. S. (1978). *Patterns of Adjustment*, New York, McGraw Hill Kogakusha Ltd.

Little John, M.T. (1967). 'Creativity and Masculinity and Feminity in Ninth Graders'. *Perceptual and Motor Skills*, 25, 737-743.

Mackinon, D.W. (1961a). *Identifying and Developing Creativity*: *Selection and Educational Differentiation.* University of California, (a) 75-89.

Mackinnon, D.W. (1961b). 'The Study of Creativity and Creativity in Architects', in *Conference on the Creative Person.* Barkeley, University of California.

Mackinnon, D.W. (1962). 'The Personality Correlates of Creativity: A Study of American Architects'. Referred in G.S. Nielson (Ed). *Proceeding of 14th International Congress of Applied Psychology*, Copenhagen. Vol. 2.

McClelland, D.C. (1956). 'The Calculated Risk: An Aspect of Scientific Performance'. *The* 1955 *University of Utah Research Conference on the Identification of Creative Scientific Talent.* Salt Lake City, University of Utah Press.

Mcclelland, D.C. 'Issues in the Identification of Talent', *Talent and Society*, (Ed. D.C. McClelland). Princeton, Van Nostrand.

McClaund, J.C. (1962). Referred in *Psychology for Classroom* by Johanna Turner, Methuen, London, pp. 79-96.

Menemar, Q. (1958). 'On Growth Measurement', *Educ. Psychol. Measmt.*, 18, 47-55.

Madaus, George, F. (1967). 'Divergent Thinking and Intelligence: Another Look at a Controversial Question'. *Journal of Education Measurement*, 4(4), 227-235.

Madnawat, A.V. (1986). 'A Study of Creativity in Relation to Intelligence and Manifest Anxiety of Higher Secondary School Boys. Unpublished Ph.D. Thesis, University of Rajsthan, Jaipur.

Mar'l, S.K. (1971). 'Creativity of American and Arab Rural Youth: A Cross-cultural study'. *Dissertation Abstracts International*, 31, 12 6407-A.

Marsh, R.W. (1964). 'A Statistical Re-analysis of Getzels and Jackson's data', *Brit. J. educ. Psychol.*, 34, 91-93.

Martynowicz, Emilia, (1965-73). Nicholas Copernicus University, Torun, Poland. Cf. *Psychological Abstract* No. 1329, Vol. 65, No. 1, January, 1981.

Mednick, S.A. (1962). 'The Associative Basis of the Creative Process'. *Psychological Review*, 69, 220-232.

Mehdi, Baqur (1973a). *Manual of Verbal Test of Creativity*. Published by Mrs. Q. Fatima, Aligarh.

Mehdi, Baqer (1973b). *Manual of Non-verbal Test of Creativity*, Published by Mrs. Qamar Fatima, Aligrah.

Mendick, S.A. (1964). 'Continual Association as a Function of Level of Creativity and Types of Verbal Stimulus'. *Journal of Abnormal and Social Psychology*, 69, 511-515.

Middents, G.J. (1968). 'Relationship of Creativity and Anxiety'. *Dissertation Abstracts*, 28, 7, 25652-A.

Mihalevici, R. *et al.* (1973). 'Individual differences in the Genesis of young Children's Creativity'. Cf. Sharma, K.N. *Dynamics of Creativity*, National Psychological Corporation, Agra.

Mohsin, S.M. (1984). *Research Methods in Behavioural Science*. Calcutta, Orient Longman.

Moore, O.K. (1961). 'Orthographic Symbols and the Pre-school Child: A New Approach'. New Educational Ideals. *Second Minnesota Conference on Gifted Children*. Minneapolis, University of Minnesota.

Moore, R. (1966). 'The Relation of Intelligence to Creativity', *J. Res. in Music Educ.*, 14, 143-253. Cf. Butcher, H.J. (1970).

Morgan, D. N. (1953). 'Creativity Today'. *Journal of Aesthetic Art and Criticism*, 12, 1-24.

Munsterberg, E. and P.R. Mussen (1953). 'The Personality Structure of Art Students'. *Joural of Personality*. 21, 457-466.

Murphy, G. (1958). *Human Potentialities*, N.Y. Basic Books.

Nair, M. (1976). 'Personality Characteristics of Creative High School Pupils'. Master's thesis, Educ. Kerala University.

Nagia, S. (1977). Referred in *Creativity in Education* by Passi B.I. Sansanwal, D.N. and Jarial, G.S. 1982, Agra, National Psychological Corporation.

Neufeld, J.J. (1964). 'The Relationship of Creative Thinking Abilities to the Academic Achievement of Adolescents'. *Dissertation Abstracts*. 25, 3404.

Northway, M.L. and M.C. Brooks (1956). 'Creativity and Socio-economic Status in Children'. *Gifted Child Quarter*, 1, 540-547.

Oden, M.H. (1968). 'The Fulfilment of Promise: 40 year Follow up of the Terman Gifted Group.' *Genetic Psychology Monograph*, 3-93. Cf. Sharma K.N. (1979).

Pandey, M.S. (1986). Motivational determinants of Creativity. Proceedings of 74th Session of Indian Science Congress.

Pandit, R. (1977). A Study of Creativity in relation to Adjustment, Socio-economic Status and Scholastic Achievement of the Students, Unpublished M. Ed. Dissertation, Indore University.

Paradowski, W. (1967). 'Effect of Curiosity on Incidental Learning'. *Journal of Educational Behaviour.* 52, 117-125.

Parnes, S. J., and E.A. Brunelle (1967). 'The Literature of Creativity', Part-I', *J. Creative Behav.* I, 52-109. Cf. Butcher, H. J. (1970).

Parker, (1963). Cf. Sinha, P. 'Effect of Home Environment and School Climate on Authoritarianism, Creativity and Fear of Failure'. 1980, Ph.D. Thesis, Patna University.

Passi, B.K. (1962). 'A Factorial Study of Creativity, Intelligence and Scholastic Achievement'. *Psychological Studies,* 7, 1, 1-9.

Pathak, P. (1962). 'Experimental Study of Creativity and Intelligence and School Achievement'. *Psychological Studies,* 7, 1-9.

Peney, Henry and Carol Horrocks, (1967). 'Creativity in a Troop of Low Average Intelligence Boy Scouts'. *Adolescence,* 26, 231-241.

Piddington, Ralph (1950). *An Introduction to Social Anthropology,* Edinburg, Oliver, and Boyd, Cf. Sharma, K.N. (1979).

Popescu Neveanu, Paul and Cornelia Facaoaru (1972). 'On the Relation between Intelligence and Creativity: Creativity as a Dimension of Personaltiy'. *Revista de Psichologic,* 18 (3), 301-314.

Prados, M. (1944). 'Rorschach Studies on Artists—Painters'. *Rorschach Research Exchange,* 8, 178-183.

Prakash, A.O. (1966). 'Understanding the Fourth Grade Slump: A Study of Creative Thinking Abilities of Indian Children'. Master's Dissertation, University of Minnesota.

Pramesh, C.R. (1970). 'Value Orientations of Creative Persons'. *Psychological Studies,* 15, 2, 108-112.

Pulaski, M.A.S. (1974). 'The Rich Rewards of Make Believe'. *Psychology Today,* 7(8), 68-74.

Querashi, A.N. (1983). 'A Study of Creativity in Relation to Intelligence, Manifest Anxiety and Level of Aspiration of High School Girls'. Ph.D. Thesis, Agra University, Agra.

Raina, M.K. (1968). 'A Study of Some Correlates of Creativity in Indian Students'. Doctoral Dissertation, University of Rajasthan.

Raina, M.K. (1971). 'Verbal and Non-verbal Creative Thinking Ability: A Study in Sex Differences'. *Journal of Education and Psychology,* 29(3), 175-179.

Rapaport, D. (1960). The Structure of Psycho-analytic Theory: A Systematizing attempt. *Psychol. Issues. Monogr,* 6, New York, International University Press.

Rawat, M.S. and Agarwal (1977). 'A Study of Creative Thinking with Reference to Intelligence, Age, Sex, Cammunities and Income Groups'. *Indian Psychological Review,* 14(2), 36-40.

Razik, T.M.A. (1964). 'An Investigation of Creative Thinking Among College Students'. *Dissertation Abstracts,* 24, 7, 2775.

Rhodes, M. (1961). An Analysis of Creativity. *Phi Delta Kappan*, 42, 305-310.

Riaz, Mohnazir (1979). 'A Study of Intelligence Creativity Distinction and their Relationship with Academic Achievement'. Pakistan Psycho logical Studies, Vol. 3, 58-70 Cf. *Psychological Abstract* No. 4349, Aug. 1981.

Richmond, Bert, O (1971). Creative and Cognitive Abilities of White and Negro Children. *Journal of Negro Educatian*, 40(2), 111-116.

Ripple, E.E. and F.B. May, (1962). 'Caution in Comparing Creativity and I.Q.', *Psychological Reports*, 10(1), 229-230.

Roe, A. (1951). 'The Personality of Artists'. *Educational Psychological Monograph*, 43, 121-239.

Roe, A. (1952). *The Making of a Scientist*. New York, Dodd, Mead and Co.

Roe, Anne (1973). Cf. *Dynamics of Creativity*. Sharma, K.N. Department of Psychology, University of Rajasthan, Jaipur, National Psychological Corporation, Agra.

Rogers, C.R. (1961). *On Becoming a Person*, Boston Houghton Mifflin.

Roger, C.R. and McGruire (1967). Referred in *Psychology for the Classroom* by Turner, J. Methuen, London.

Rossman. J. (1931). *The Psychology of the Inventor*. Washington, D. C., Inventors Publishing Co.

Rossman, Betty, B. and Harry, F. Gollob (1975). 'Comparison of Social Judgements of Creativity and Intelligence'. *Journal of Personality and Social Psychology*, 31(2), 271, 281.

Runner Associate (1954). *Runner Studies of Attitude Patterns*. Golden, Colo.

Sajid, S.M. (1984). 'Creativity and Intelligence'. Unpublished Ph.D. Thesis, Patna University, Patna Bihar.

Sallery, Robert D. (1968). 'Artistic Expression and Self-Description with Arabs and Canadian Students'. *Journal of Social Psychology*, 76, 2, 273-274.

Sansanwal D. N. and G. Singh Jarial (1981). Referred in *Creativity in Education* by B. K. Passi, D. N. Sansawal and G. S. Jarial, P. 14, 1982.

Shafer, C.E. and Anne Anastasi (1968). 'A Biological Inventory for Identifying Creativity in Adolescent Boys'. *Journal of Applied Psychology*, 52, 42-48.

Shapiro, R J. (1965). 'The Integrating of Remotely Associated Concept as a Process in Scientific Creativity', *Psychologia Africana*, II, 40-48. Cf. Butcher H.J. (1970).

Shapiro R.J. (1966). 'The Identification of Creative Research Scientists', *Psychologia Africana*-II, 99-132. Cf. Butcher, H.J. (1970).

Sharan, P. (1986). 'A study of Familial and Personalistic Under-currents of

Creativity. Unpublished Ph.D. Thesis, Patna University, Patna, Bihar.

Sharma, (1974) Cf Madnavat, A.V. (1986). 'A Study of Creativity in Relation to Intelligence & Manifest Anxiety of Higher Secondary School Boys'. Unpublished Ph.D. Thesis, University of Rajasthan, Jaipur.

Sharma, A.K. (1980). 'Creativity and its Components as Affected by Socio-economic Status and Personality. *Experiments in Education* 8, (7), 129-133.

Sharma, K.N. (1979). *Dynamics of Creativity*, Agra, Nat. Psy. Corp.

Simpson, R.M. (1922). 'Creative Imagination'. *American Journal of Psychology*, 33, 234-243.

Singh, R. *et al.* (1970). 'Creativity as Related to Intelligence, Achievement and Security-Insecurity. *Indian Psycholaoical Review*, 14(3), 84-87.

Singh, R. (1975). 'A Study of Creativity Among Tenth Class Students in Relation to their Adjustment and Sex. Unpublished M.L.T. Dissertation, Punjab University.

Singh, R.B., Sudha Mathur and Shashi Saxena (1977). 'Creativity as Related to Intelligence, Achievement and Security-Insecurity'. *Indian Psychological Review*, Vol. 14(2) 84-88.

Singh R.J. (1978). 'The Psychological Make-up and Sociological Background of Creative and Non-creative Student Teachers'. *Indian Educational Review*, 13, (4) 119, 123.

Singh R.J. (1980a). 'Teacher Creativity and Family Background: A Study of Relationship'. *Asian Journal of Psychology and Education*, 6, (3). 42-48. Cf. *Psychological Abstract* No. 2033, 68, July, 1982.

Singh R.J. (1980b). 'Personality Adjustment of Creative and Non-creative Student Teachers in India. *Indian Educational Review*. 15, (4). 44-56.

Snyder, B. (1967). 'Creative Studies in Science and Engineering', *University Quarterly*, 21 (2), 275-280.

Spearman, C. (1930). *Creative Mind*, London, Cambridge University Press.

Spearman, C.E. (1931). 'Our Need of Some Science in Place of the Word intelligence'. *J. Educ. Psychol.*, 30, 1-16.

Spotts, J.V. and B. Mackler (1967). Relationship of Field Dependent and Field Independent Cognitive Style to Creative Test Performance, *Perceptual and Motor Skills*, 24(1) 239-268.

Springbelt, B.M. *et al.* (1957). 'An Approach to the Measurement of Creative Thinking'. *Canadian Journal of Psychology*, ii, 9-20.

Srivastava, L. (1978). 'Creativity as a Function of Birth Order, Socio-Economic Status and Personality Types'. *Journal of Education and Psychology*, 41, (3), 113-117.

Stein, M.I. (1960) *Creativity and Individual*, New York, Free Press.

Stone, Mary A. and David P. Ausbel (1969). The Intersituational Generality of Formal Thought. *Journal of Genetic Psy.*, 115(2), 169-180. Cf. *Psychological Abstract*, Vol. 44, No. 6, Abstract No. 8176, June 1970.

Strauss, M.E. and M.A. Strauss (1968). 'Family Roles and Sex Differences in Creativity of Children in Bombay and Minneapolis'. *Journal of Marriage and the family,* 30(1), 46-53. Cf. Sharma, K. N. (1979).

Taft, R.A. (1961). 'A Psychological Assessment of Professional Actor', *Genetic Psychological Monograph.*

Taylor, C.W. (1955). *The Identification of Creative Scientific Talent.* Salt Lake City, Utah, University of Utah, Press.

Taylor, C.W. and F. Barron (1963). *Scientific Creativity.* N.Y. Robert E. Krieger Publishing Co., Huntington.

Thorndike, R.L. (1963). 'Some Methodological Issues in the Study of Creativity'. *Proceedings of the* 1962 *International Conference on Testing Problems.* Princetone, N.J., Educational Testing Service.

Thurstone, L.L. (1955). 'The Differential Growth of Mental Abilities', Chapel Hill, North Carolina. *Report of Univ. of N. Carolina Psychometric Laboratory* No. 14. Cf. Butcher, H.J. (1970).

Torrance E.P. (1959). Personality Studies of Highly Creative Children (Explorations in Creative Thinking in the Early School Years. No. 9) *Research Memo BER*-59-12. Minneapolis, Bureau of Educational Research, of Minnesota.

Torrance, E.P. (1960). 'Educational Achievement of the Highly Intelligent and Highly Creative : Eight Partial Replications of the Getzels-Jackson Study', (*Research Memorandum BER*-60-18) Bureau of Educ. Research, Univ. of Minnesota. Cf. Butcher H.J. (1970).

Torrance, E.P. (1962). *Guiding Creative Talent.* N.D., Prentice Hall of India Ltd.

Torrance, E.P. (1965). *Rewarding Creative Behaviour.* Englewood Cliffs. N.J., Prentice-Hall.

Torrance E.P. (1966). *Nature of Creative talents : Theory into Practice,* 5, 168-173.

Torrance, E.P. (1967). 'Give the Devil His Dues', in J.C. Gowan, G.D. Demos and E.P. Torrance's *Creativity : Its Educational Implications.* N.Y., Wiley.

Torrance E.P. (1969). *Comparative Studies in Creativity in Children, Educational Leadership.* 27, 146, 148.

Varela, J.A. (1969). 'Elaboration of Guilford's S.I. Model', *Psychological Review,* 76, 332-336.

Verma, L.K. (1980). 'A Study of Locus of Control of High and Low Creative School Students, at Different Levels of Socio-economic Status'. *Journal of Education and Psychology,* 38, (2), 99-104.

Verma O.P. (1979). 'Personality Traits of Creative Students in Biology'. *Education,* 1, (6).

Vernon, P.E. (1964b). 'Creativity and Intelligence'. *Educ. Res.,* 6, 163-169.

Vernon, P.E. (1967). 'A Cross-Cultural Study of Creativity Tests with 11 Year Old Boys, *New Research in Education,* 1, 135-146.

Vidyarthi, L.P. (1968). Cultural Change in the Tribes of India. Presidential address, Sec. of Anthropology and Archaeology, 65th session of the Indian Science Congress Assn.

Vijay Lakshmi J.C. (1980). 'Academic Achievement and Socio-economic Status as Predictors of Creative Talent'. *Journal of Psychology Resources*, 24, (1).

Vinacke, W.E. (1960). *The Psychology of Thinking*. N.Y., McGraw Hill.

Wallach, M.A. and Kogan (1965). *Modes of Thinking in Young Children : A Study of Creativity Intelligence Distinction*. New York, Holt, Rinehart and Winston.

Wallas, G. (1926). *The Art of Thought*. N.Y., Harcourt, Brace.

Ward, W.C. et al. (1970). *Motivation and Capacity in Children's Creativity*. Princeton, N.J., ETS Bulletin, 70-89.

Ward, W.C. and P.W. Cox (1974). 'A Field Study of Non-verbal Creativity'. *Journal of Personality*, 42 (2), 202-219.

Weiman, Regina, M. (1975). 'The Relationship of Creativity to Intelligence and Functional Fixedness'. *Dissertation Abstracts International*, 35 (12-A, Pt. 1), 7667.

Weisberg, P.S. and K.J. Springer, (1961). *Environmental Factors Influencing Creative Function in Gifted Children*. Cincinneti, Deptt. of Psychiatry, Cinicinnati General Hospital.

White, Leslie A. (1959). *The Evolution of Culture*. N.Y., McGraw-Hill.

White, R.W. (1963). 'Ego and Reality in Psycho-analysis Theory : A Proposal Regarding Independent Ego Energies. *Psychol. Issues.*, Mongr. No.11, New York, International Universities Press.

Williams, F.E. (1965). 'Practice and Reinforcement as Training Factor in Creative Performance'. Doctoral Dissertation, University of Utah.

Wilson, R.N. (1954). 'Poetic Creativity, Process and Personality'. *Psychiatry*, 17, 2, 193-196.

Worthen, B.R. (1968). 'Discovery and Expository Task Presentation in Elementray Mathematics'. *Journal of Educational Psychology*, 59, 1-13.

Yamamoto, K. (1960). 'Further Analysis of Ask-and-Guess Tests'. *Research Memorandum BER*-60. Minneapolis, Minnesota Bureau of Educational Research, University of Minnesota. Cf. Butcher, H.J. (1970).

Yamamoto, K. (1964a). 'Role of Creative Thinking and Intelligence in High School Achievement'. *Psychol. Rep.* 14, 783-789. Cf. Butcher, H.J. (1970).

Yamamoto, K. (1964b). 'Threshold of Intelligence in Academic Achievement of Highly Creative Students', *J. Exper. Educ.*, 32, 401-404. Cf. Butcher, H.J. (1970).

Yamamoto, K. (1964c). 'Further Analysis of the Role of Creative Thinking in High School Achievement', *J. Psychol.*, 58, 277-283.

Yamamoto, K. (1964d). Creative Thinking: Some thoughts on Research on exceptional Children, 30, 403-410.

Yamamoto, K. (1965). 'Effects of Restriction of Range and Test Unreliability on Correlation between Measures of Intelligence and Creative Thinking'. *British Journal of Educational Psychology*, 35, 300-305.

Zeleny, L.D. (1956). 'Validity of Socio-metric Hypothesis : The Function of Creativity in Interpersonal and Group Relations.' *Sociometry*, 18, 439-449.

NAMES INDEX

NAMES INDEX

SUBJECT INDEX